Managing
Health Services

Cases in Organization Design
and Decision Making

Managing
Health Services

Cases in Organization Design
and Decision Making

Deborah E. Bender
with Julie Curkendall
and Heather Manning

Health Administration Press, Chicago, Illinois
AUPHA Press, Washington, D.C.

AUPHA
HAP

Your board, staff, or clients may also benefit from this book's insight. For more information on quantity discounts, contact the Health Administration Press marketing manager at 312/424-9470.

04 03 02 01 00   5 4 3 2 1

Library of Congress Cataloging-in-Publication Data

Bender, Deborah.
    Managing health services: cases in organization design and decision
    making / by Deborah E. Bender, Heather Manning, and Julie
    Curkendall.
        p. cm.
    ISBN 1-56793-125-1 (alk. paper)
    1. Health facilities—Administration—Case studies. 2. Health facilities—
Administration—Decision making—Case studies.
I. Manning, Heather. II. Curkendall, Julie. III. Title.
    RA971 .B36 2000
    362.1'068—dc21

                                                        99-089904
                                                            CIP

The paper used in this publication meets the minimum requirements of American National Standards for Information Sciences—Permanence of Paper for Printed Library Materials, ANSI Z39.48–1984. ♾ ™

Health Administration Press   AUPHA
A division of the Foundation of   730 11th Street., NW
    the American College of   4th Floor
    Healthcare Executives   Washington, DC 20001
One North Franklin Street, Suite 1700   202/638-1448
Chicago, IL 60606-3491
312/424-2800

Contents

vii

Acknowledgments

THE AUTHOR WISHES to acknowledge the creative contributions of the student authors whose cases were the basis for those included in this book. Thanks, too, are offered to the students' internship preceptors—practicing professionals who gave generously of their time and experience to demonstrate applications of theory to practice in the health services setting.

Special thanks are due, as well, to the substantial energies, organizational skills, and unflagging good humor of Heather Manning and Julie Curkendall, graduate assistants to this project. Without their perseverance, this book would continue to be only a good idea.

Thanks also are bestowed on Martha Arnold, of UNC-Chapel Hill's Center for Teaching and Learning, whose expertise in classroom curricula innovation nurtured an idea until it became a plan.

Thanks, too, to the staff of Health Administration Press for their even-handed help in producing this book. With their help, the onerous was almost enjoyable.

Finally, I want to thank my spouse, John Curry, and my children, Sean, Daniel, and Kirsten, for their enthusiastic support of this project—"Go, Dr. Mom!"

ix

Foreword

PETER DRUCKER ONCE said, "Young people need to learn organizations the way our forefathers learned farming." Deborah Bender and her colleagues and students have taken this advice to heart. The series of management cases prepared by students and organized by managerial topic and healthcare setting is an attempt to illustrate the fundamentals of management to students who are just beginning their managerial career. While it is always tempting to present the complexity and detail of the many unrelenting challenges that face managers, there also is a need to focus on fundamentals and the illustration of these fundamentals in a variety of healthcare settings.

Perhaps the importance of the need to focus on the fundamentals is best illustrated by a story told by Don Berwick, president and CEO of the Institute for Healthcare Improvement. His comments were published as a preface to a book published by the Joint Commission on Accreditation of Healthcare Organizations in 1991 entitled *Striving Toward Improvement: Six Hospitals in Search of Quality.*

Don Berwick had climbed Mount Rainier three times before and was about to launch his fourth effort. On this climb he was joined by a small group and guided by Phil Ershler—a world-class mountaineer who has stood on the summits of Everest and K2. "Mount Rainier in the state of Washington is no Everest, but is a serious mountain containing more glacier mass than any other mountain in the lower 48 states. Mount Rainier's summit is 14,410 feet and the surrounding air has an air pressure only half that at sea level," described Berwick. In three previous ascents, Berwick had climbed to the 10,000-foot mark. He had found each climb to be a draining experience and had arrived thoroughly exhausted.

In preparation of his fourth climb, Berwick recalls that Ershler told the group: "First, we are going to learn some methods.... I am going to teach you two things...how to walk and how to breathe." Berwick recalls laughing; he said, "We thought we were here to learn technique—crampons, ice axes, crevasse rescue, not walking and breathing." But, six hours later, Berwick and his fellow climbers were no longer laughing. Ershler had done exactly what he had said. "The habitual, unconscious actions of walking and breathing had been transformed into self-conscious, planned, placed, comprehended, and practiced tools for our success on the mountain," Berwick recounted. "We studied equipment, the shape of snow, the position of our lips and our arms, the 'rest step', and the distances between us. Walking and breathing had become...a constellation of a dozen or more small and purposeful parts, each designed and each defined by experience, theory, and logic. Together, these learned parts added up to a new way—a transformation of methods."

Managing Health Services is a book about "walking and breathing." The cases explore the kinds of situations and challenges that managers confront every day in a range of healthcare organizations. Through this kind of careful exploration, we hope to be able to hone the skills of emerging managers and leaders to walk and breathe in the increasingly challenging world of health services management.

Arnold D. Kaluzny, PH.D.
Professor of Health Policy and Administration and
Director of the Public Health Leadership Program,
School of Public Health and
Senior Research Fellow,
Cecil G. Sheps Center for Health Services Research,
University of North Carolina at Chapel Hill

Introduction

WHEN I WAS in college, my Dad offered me a unique lesson in logic. He attempted to prove to me that a loaf of bread is logically the mother of a locomotive. "A loaf of bread," he said, "is a necessity. A locomotive is an invention. And, everyone knows that necessity is the mother of invention. By simple analogy," he concluded, "a loaf of bread is the mother of a locomotive." My dad was an engineer, not a philosopher.

The idea of developing a casebook was an invention that I hoped would respond to a necessity. In 1996, when I began this project, I was—or rather, my students were—frustrated at the lack of cases tailored to illustrate specific management concepts for students who are embarking on management careers. The majority of cases that were available were long and complex. I wanted a set of cases that were demonstrative of the conceptual point at hand, but ones that could also stimulate students to delve into their own work experience to identify similar examples.

This casebook, then, is an invention that grew out of that frustration or, rather, that necessity. The invitation to students to try their hand at writing cases for the casebook was only a logical extension of their earlier involvement. But more importantly, developing cases based on immediate past experience ensures that problems addressed are consistent with those of today's healthcare managers and those that these students could encounter later in their careers.

Each student in the class had just completed a 12-week internship in a health service setting. They were enthusiastic and full of answers. It seemed the only ingredient missing was a good question. We set out to try it together. I asked, "In your internship, can you remember one particular moment in which a manager, your preceptor, or someone else made a decision, took a step that was outstanding in its importance?" I added that it was not important whether the decision was a good one or a bad one, but rather that the decision—or nondecision—was one that significantly influenced the quality of care offered by the agency and the well-being of its employees. The students lit up; each of them had something to say. First, they talked to each other. They crystallized their ideas. They analyzed the chain of events that had occurred. They rechecked details with a workplace colleague. Then, they wrote the cases.

The cases selected are based on actual managerial problems that the students observed during their internships. Through their participative roles, the students had a unique opportunity to view the organizations' function from the inside, despite their relatively objective temporary position. These real-world situations became points of departure for developing hypothetical cases that became, in turn, the basis for the more fully developed cases presented in this book.

Each case scenario is structured around one primary organizational design topic, such as organizational structure or leadership. However, the cases include more than one issue given that many organizational structure and behavior elements are closely intertwined. Consequently, each case touches on one or more additional organizational design sub-topic. Various health service settings are presented here, which reflect the growing range and complexity of services offered today. Organizational settings range from large hospital systems to community health departments to government entities, while geographical settings include rural areas, small college towns, and sprawling metropolitan areas.

The diversity of organizational and geographical settings communicates two points:

1. Regardless of setting, health services experience tension and change in a similar way.
2. Regardless of setting, organizational structure and behavior elements influence how situations occur and are resolved. The setting, however, affects organizational structure and behavior.

Paying attention to the effect of the organizational design on the morale and motivation of its employees and front-line, mid-line, and strategic management allows managers to alter or reconfigure design components in ways that are responsive to the professional and personnel needs of employees. Structure is more mutable than personality.

To guide the reader, the following symbols will be used:

- The square refers to the primary focus of the case—organizational theory, structure, and behavior.
- The diamond refers to the secondary focus of the case.
- The circle refers to the organizational setting—hospital, health center, physician group practice, government program, etc.

Each case is organized in the following manner:

- Focused Topic Description
- Learning/Teaching Objective(s)
- Background and Case Overview
- Organizational Problem
- Questions for Discussion

A series of tables designed to facilitate discussion and application of each case to a variety of health settings is provided within. Tables 1 and 2 illustrate how each case exemplifies and fits into the rubric of the concepts presented in the textbooks *Health Care Management: Organization Design and Behavior, Fourth Edition* by Stephen M. Shortell and Arnold D. Kaluzny and *The Well-Managed Healthcare Organization, Fourth Edition* by John R. Griffith. Table 1 categorizes each case under the following main concepts in *Health Care Management*:

- Motivating, leading, and negotiating
- Operating the technical system
- Renewing the organization

Table 2, on the other hand, lists the cases under the following concepts addressed in *The Well-Managed Healthcare Organization:*

- Governing: responding to the environment
- Caring: quality of clinical service
- Learning: the information and support needs of organizations

Lastly, Table 3 provides an organized, by-setting list of the cases.

Possible solutions to each case's Questions for Discussion section as well as tips on how to encourage students to write cases, are provided for the instructor in the accompanying Instructor's Manual.

Table 1 Case Illustration of Concepts in *Health Care Management: Organization Design and Behavior, Fourth Edition*

Motivating, Leading, and Negotiating	Operating the Technical System	Renewing the Organization
Primary Focus: Communication Help Is on the Way! Or Maybe Not Hospice Goes Hollywood *Primary Focus: Conflict and Negotiation* Communicating Toward a Winning Team Taking Care of Business at Graceland Memorial Hospital *Primary Focus: Group Behavior and Teams* Piecing It Together *Primary Focus: Leadership* Decisions, Decisions Urgent Relief *Primary Focus: Motivation* Hurry-Home Home Care Merit Bonuses at Piney Neurology *Primary Focus: Power and Control* CFO versus CEO What Went Wrong?	*Primary Focus: Decision Making* The Ax Man Cometh To Have or Not to Have Centralized Scheduling *Primary Focus: Organizational Effectiveness* Organizational Effectiveness at U.S. Better Housing Department Staying Alive Where's the Paper? *Primary Focus: Organizational Size* It's Alive! Wham! No Standardization *Primary Focus: Organizational Structure (Centralization)* "I Can't Do It All!" Keeping Spirits High *Primary Focus: Organizational Structure (Complexity)* A Neverending Battle Family Matters at Cariño Who's the Boss? *Primary Focus: Organizational Structure (Formalization)* And In This Corner... A New Male Supervisor *Primary Focus: Organizational Structure (Socialization)* Gaining Access to the Hispanic Community *Primary Focus: Technology* A Double Standard We're Not Gonna Take It Anymore	*Primary Focus: Customers and the Environmental Domain* Stop the Presses! The Rocky Road to Patient Satisfaction at Leonard-Griggs *Primary Focus: Environment* Declining Census and Its Effects on Motivation and Morale Patient Satisfaction Up In Smoke Strategies for Serving an Atypical Patient Population *Primary Focus: Organizational Change* A Focus on Departmental Downsizing Beach Memorial Hospital *Primary Focus: Organizational Culture* The Fine Balance Global Culture in the Workplace No Time to Waste Parlez-Vous Français? *Primary Focus: Organizational Life Cycles* Student Coalition for Immigrants and Farmworkers

Table 1 Continued

Motivating, Leading, and Negotiating	Operating the Technical System	Renewing the Organization
Secondary Focus: Communication And In This Corner... Communicating Toward a Winning Team A Double Standard Global Culture in the Workplace Parlez-Vous Français? Piecing It Together We're Not Gonna Take It Anymore Who's the Boss?	*Secondary Focus: Decision Making* A Focus on Departmental Downsizing A Neverending Battle Merit Bonuses at Piney Neurology CFO versus CEO	*Secondary Focus: Customers and the Environmental Domain* Patient Satisfaction Up In Smoke Where's the Paper?
Secondary Focus: Conflict and Negotiation Beach Memorial Hospital	*Secondary Focus: Organizational Effectiveness* Hurry-Home Home Care Wham! No Standardization	*Secondary Focus: Environment* Gaining Access to the Hispanic Community Decisions, Decisions Stop the Presses!
Secondary Focus: Group Behavior and Teams None	*Secondary Focus: Organizational Size* None	*Secondary Focus: Organizational Change* Taking Care of Business at Graceland Memorial Hospital The Ax Man Cometh Family Matters at Cariño
Secondary Focus: Leadership "I Can't Do It All!"	*Secondary Focus: Organizational Structure* Help Is on the Way! Or Maybe Not Hospice Goes Hollywood The Rocky Road to Patient Satisfaction at Leonard-Griggs	
Secondary Focus: Motivation Declining Census and Its Effects on Motivation and Morale		*Secondary Focus: Organizational Culture* Strategies for Serving an Atypical Patient Population
Secondary Focus: Power and Control None	*Secondary Focus: Organizational Structure (Centralization)* To Have or Not to Have Centralized Scheduling	*Secondary Focus: Organizational Life Cycles* Staying Alive
	Secondary Focus: Organizational Structure (Complexity) The Fine Balance It's Alive! Student Coalition for Immigrants and Farmworkers	
	Secondary Focus: Technology None	

Table 2 Case Illustration of Concepts in *The Well-Managed Healthcare Organization, Fourth Edition*

Governing: Responding to the Environment	Caring: Quality of Clinical Services	Learning: Information and Support Needs of Organization
Primary Focus: Customers and Environmental Domain Stop the Presses! The Rocky Road to Patient Satisfaction at Leonard-Griggs *Primary Focus: Environment* Declining Census and Its Effects on Motivation and Morale Patient Satisfaction Up In Smoke Strategies for Serving an Atypical Patient Population *Primary Focus: Leadership* Decisions, Decisions Urgent Relief *Primary Focus: Organizational Life Cycles* Student Coalition for Immigrants and Farmworkers *Primary Focus: Organizational Size* It's Alive! Wham! No Standardization *Primary Focus: Organizational Structure (Centralization)* "I Can't Do It All!" Keeping Spirits High *Primary Focus: Organizational Structure (Complexity)* A Neverending Battle Family Matters at Cariño Who's the Boss? *Primary Focus: Organizational Structure (Formalization)* And In This Corner... A New Male Supervisor	*Primary Focus: Communication* Help Is on the Way! Or Maybe Not Hospice Goes Hollywood *Primary Focus: Conflict and Negotiation* Communicating Toward a Winning Team Taking Care of Business at Graceland Memorial Hospital *Primary Focus: Group Behavior and Teams* Piecing It Together *Primary Focus: Motivation* Hurry-Home Home Care Merit Bonuses at Piney Neurology *Primary Focus: Organizational Change* A Focus on Departmental Downsizing Beach Memorial Hospital *Primary Focus: Organizational Culture* The Fine Balance Global Culture in the Workplace Parlez-Vous Français? No Time to Waste *Primary Focus: Technology* A Double Standard We're Not Gonna Take It Anymore	*Primary Focus: Decision Making* The Ax Man Cometh To Have or Not to Have Centralized Scheduling *Primary Focus: Organizational Effectiveness* Organizational Effectiveness at U.S. Better Housing Department Staying Alive Where's the Paper? *Primary Focus: Power and Control* CFO versus CEO What Went Wrong? *Primary Focus: Technology* A Double Standard We're Not Gonna Take It Anymore

Table 2 Continued

Governing: Responding to the Environment	Caring: Quality of Clinical Services	Learning: Information and Support Needs of Organization
Secondary Focus: Customers and Environmental Domain Where's the Paper?	*Secondary Focus: Communication* Communicating Toward a Winning Team	*Secondary Focus: Decision Making* Merit Bonuses at Piney Neurology
Secondary Focus: Environment Stop the Presses! Decisions, Decisions Gaining Access to the Hispanic Community	Piecing It Together Global Culture in the Workplace Parlez-Vous Français? Who's the Boss? And In This Corner...	A Focus on Departmental Downsizing A Neverending Battle CFO versus CEO
Secondary Focus: Leadership "I Can't Do It All!" What Went Wrong?	We're Not Gonna Take It Anymore A Double Standard	*Secondary Focus: Organizational Effectiveness* Hurry-Home Home Care No Time to Waste Wham! No Standardization
Secondary Focus: Organizational Life Cycles Staying Alive	*Secondary Focus: Conflict and Negotiation* Beach Memorial Hospital Organizational Effectiveness at U.S. Better Housing Department	*Secondary Focus: Power and Control* None
Secondary Focus: Organizational Size None		*Secondary Focus: Technology* None
Secondary Focus: Organizational Structure (Formalization) Hospice Goes Hollywood Help Is on the Way! Or Maybe Not The Rocky Road to Patient Satisfaction at Leonard-Griggs	*Secondary Focus: Group Behavior and Teams* None	
	Secondary Focus: Motivation Declining Census and Its Effects on Motivation and Morale Urgent Relief Keeping Spirits High	
Secondary Focus: Organizational Structure (Centralization) To Have or Not to Have Centralized Scheduling	*Secondary Focus: Organizational Change* Taking Care of Business at Graceland Memorial Hospital The Ax Man Cometh Family Matters at Cariño	
Secondary Focus: Organizational Structure (Complexity) The Fine Balance Student Coalition for Immigrants and Farmworkers It's Alive!	*Secondary Focus: Organizational Culture* Strategies for Serving an Atypical Patient Population	

Table 3 Case by Setting

Organizational Setting	Case Title
Alliance	A Neverending Battle
Assisted Living Facility	Where's the Paper?
Consulting Firm	No Time to Waste
County Health Department	What Went Wrong?
Department of Family Medicine	It's Alive!
Diagnostic Center	A New Male Supervisor
Foundation	We're Not Gonna Take It Anymore
Government	The Fine Balance
Government	Organizational Effectiveness at U.S. Better Housing Department
Health Services Research Center	Parlez-Vous Français?
Health Services Research Center	Piecing It Together
HMO	"I Can't Do It All!"
Home Health Agency	Hurry-Home Home Care
Home Health Agency	Staying Alive
Hospice, not-for-profit	Hospice Goes Hollywood
Hospital, community, not-for-profit	And In This Corner...
Hospital, community, not-for-profit	Patient Satisfaction Up In Smoke
Hospital, community, not-for-profit	CFO versus CEO
Hospital, community, not-for-profit	Taking Care of Business at Graceland Memorial Hospital
Hospital, community, not-for-profit	The Ax Man Cometh
Hospital, general	Beach Memorial Hospital
Hospital, government run by Indian Health Service	Stop the Presses!
Hospital, teaching, not-for-profit	To Have or Not to Have Centralized Scheduling
Hospital, teaching	A Focus on Departmental Downsizing
Hospital, teaching	Decisions, Decisions
Hospital, teaching	Global Culture in the Workplace
Hospital, teaching	Keeping Spirits High
Hospital, teaching	Who's the Boss?
Integrated Care System	Gaining Access to the Hispanic Community
Integrated Care System	Family Matters at Cariño
Migrant Health Network, not-for-profit	Strategies for Serving an Atypical Patient Population
Migrant Health Network	Student Coalition for Immigrants and Farmworkers
MSO	The Rocky Road to Patient Satisfaction at Leonard-Griggs

Table 3 Contined

Organizational Setting	Case Title
Physician Practice	A Double Standard
Rehabilitation Center, for-profit	Declining Census and Its Effects on Motivation and Morale
Retirement community, not-for-profit	Help Is on the Way! Or Maybe Not
Specialty Clinic	Communicating Toward a Winning Team
Specialty Clinic	Merit Bonuses at Piney Neurology
State Education Network	Wham! No Standardization
Urgent Care Clinic	Urgent Relief

PART ONE

Communication

Case 1: Help Is on the Way!
Or Maybe Not

☐ *Communication*
◇ *Organizational Structure: Formalization*
◎ *Retirement Community*

FOCUSED TOPIC DESCRIPTION

This case focuses on how lack of communication within an organization can negatively affect the organization's ability to meet its goals.

LEARNING/TEACHING OBJECTIVES

- To observe how lack of communication at various levels within an organization has an adverse effect on other levels within the organization
- To learn the importance of clear job descriptions in promoting effective communication within an organization
- To understand why ongoing training and feedback mechanisms for employees are important

Ridge View Retirement Community is a private, not-for-profit continuing care retirement community in a college town in Colorado. Ridge View strives to provide a safe, healthy, and secure environment for people in their later years. The retirement community was founded 15 years ago by a group of eight elderly area residents who wanted access to a health service setting with assisted living arrangements and long-term care. They also imagined a setting that would provide quality residential living to elderly citizens. Ridge View opened with 20 residents 15 years ago; today, the number of its residents has tripled to more than 60.

Ridge View provides care to residents who live independently and to those who need assistance to meet their daily needs. Ridge View provides two levels of care beyond independent living. The least dependent, and newest, level of care available is Assisted Living, where minimal assistance with daily activities is provided to residents. Residents who need more assistance with activities of daily living are cared for in the Health Center facility. Licensed healthcare professionals provide supervision for the residents at the Health Center in which the level of care is similar to that of other skilled nursing facilities. The Assisted Living facility was created to provide additional care for some residents and reduce healthcare costs. The intent was to continue to create a non-medical, home-like environment to which those in independent living units were accustomed and provide security for those who experienced losses.

When Assisted Living was created two years ago at Ridge View, the director of the health services department, Sandy Griffin, RN, was appointed as its administrator. Although Mrs. Griffin felt that she was already overworked and unable to allocate an appropriate amount of supervising time to each department, she reluctantly added Assisted Living to the growing list of departments at Ridge View for which she was responsible. As a condition of accepting the position, Mrs. Griffin negotiated the creation of a new administrative assistant position—Resident Services manager—that would provide her some assistance in overseeing the day-to-day operations of Assisted Living.

However, because of time pressures, the position was outlined and described only verbally; Mrs. Griffin promised that a formal job description would be forthcoming. Rather than spend time posting the job and accepting applications, Mrs. Griffin decided that it would be best to hire internally. She offered the position to Holly Roberts, the current dining room manager. Ms. Roberts had little experience or formal education in the field of assisted living, but Mrs. Griffin was convinced that Ms. Roberts's personality and demonstration of professionalism in her current leadership role made her a great candidate for the position. Although Ms. Roberts did not understand the details of the new position, she accepted the job and assumed that all would be clarified soon. She thought Mrs. Griffin seemed like a very reasonable person.

Ms. Roberts was now responsible for overseeing the Assisted Living staff—personal care assistants who have limited medical training. Medical conditions, problems, and medications are written in a notebook and checked daily by a visiting nurse. According to the policy and procedure manual, in the event of an emergency, Assisted Living staff must call a registered nurse from the Health Center who in turn is expected to respond immediately. Personal care assistants were informed of this and various other policies and procedures in a two-day training program.

During the first several months of operation, the Assisted Living unit ran smoothly. Ms. Roberts encouraged personal care assistants to talk with her about any concerns, and Mrs. Griffin and Ms. Roberts weekly discussed the status of residents and problems that have, or might have, arisen. As time went on, personal care assistants became more comfortable with their jobs and assumed more autonomy; Ms. Roberts became more relaxed in her role, as well; and administrators less frequently monitored the unit. However, because of the informal, relaxed environment that Ms. Roberts promoted, personal care assistants were less vigilant of Ridge View's policies and procedures, including procedures that detail specific roles and responsibilities that staff must take on in a medical emergency. Ms. Roberts's position description still had not been completed and administrative reporting channels still had not been specified. Unaware of the mounting problems, management continued to work on other projects.

ORGANIZATIONAL PROBLEM

Although personal care assistants were familiar with all unit policies, they found them difficult to follow. In an emergency, personal care assistants did contact registered nurses. However, they often found it difficult to locate a nurse by phone and when they did find a nurse, the nurse often informed them that the emergency was not a nurse's responsibility and instructed them to contact someone else. As a result, conflicts began to arise between the personal care assistants and the nurses, and the time necessary to get help began taking longer. The personal care assistants complained among themselves. However, no steps were taken to notify either Ms. Roberts or Mrs. Griffin of the conflicts.

Emily, Assisted Living's new part-time personal care assistant, had only been faced with a couple of emergency situations. In each event, she had called a nurse directly as instructed by her coworkers. Responses had taken as much as 20 minutes because nurses were less willing to respond to requests from personal care assistants. Emily talked about the problem with Ms. Roberts, who responded by posting a list of various phone numbers of the nurses at the Health Center.

One evening when Mrs. Griffin was walking through Assisted Living, Emily stopped her to discuss the problem. Mrs. Griffin seemed surprised and responded, "The procedure is simple. Personal care assistants are supposed to call the communications desk. The communication clerk then calls the designated nurse and records the amount of time it takes for the nurse to respond."

A surprised Emily replied, "There must have been some type of mix-up around here. Everyone has told me we should call the nurse directly." Mrs. Griffin resolved to check the policy and procedure manual and talk with her staff first thing Monday morning, but, unfortunately, she was not able to do so because the inspectors from the Department of Social Services arrived unexpectedly. The communication problem between the staffs of Assisted Living and the Health Center was once again pushed aside.

The next day during Emily's duty, Mrs. Brown, a feeble but outspoken resident, pulled her emergency cord. Emily responded within seconds and found Mrs. Brown lying on her bathroom floor. Remembering her conversation with Mrs. Griffin, Emily immediately called the communications desk: "We need a nurse in Assisted Living. Mrs. Brown has fallen and needs medical help right away!" The voice on the other end of the phone replied, "What do you want me to do about it?" A disagreement followed, then the communications clerk finally agreed to call a nurse. Emily waited patiently with Mrs. Brown, but after 15 minutes, she called the communications desk again. "She's on her way," mumbled the voice at the communications desk.

Ten minutes passed. Now, both Emily and Mrs. Brown were very angry. Emily, then, called the nurse directly who said that she was just walking out the door. Thirty minutes after the initial call to the communications desk, a perturbed nurse arrived to care for a very upset Mrs. Brown.

The following day at the resident council meeting, Mrs. Brown told her story. The resident council immediately sent a representative to Mrs. Griffin's office to demand a resolution to this inexcusable problem. Mrs. Griffin called a meeting with the director of nursing, the nursing shift supervisors, the communication manager, Emily, and Ms. Roberts to discuss and decide on means to correct the problem. Mrs. Griffin was concerned that there were other practices on the unit that are inconsistent with written policies and procedures. The need to establish consistent and clear patterns of communication seemed urgent.

QUESTIONS FOR DISCUSSION

1. What are the major sources of the communication problem at Ridge View? What adverse effect may occur? What could be done to correct these problems?
2. Give possible reasons for the confusion in understanding the procedures.
3. What suggestions do you have for formalizing the communications on the unit?
4. What steps could be taken to improve the training of the personal care assistants?

Case 2: Hospice Goes Hollywood

☐ *Communication*
◇ *Organizational Structure: Formalization*
◎ *Hospice*

FOCUSED TOPIC DESCRIPTION

This case illustrates how lack of appropriate communication among departments affects the operations of a hospice. In addition, the case explores the relationship among organizational structure, formalization, and communication.

LEARNING/TEACHING OBJECTIVE

- To develop an understanding of how communication affects work flow, productivity, and employee interactions

BACKGROUND AND CASE OVERVIEW

Hollywood Hospice is a not-for-profit, 85-bed hospice facility located in the small, but populous, town of Hollywood, California. Like all other hospices, its mission is to provide high quality palliative care to the terminally ill. Because it is located in a competitive environment that receives much media coverage, Hollywood Hospice is extremely conscious of its image. Hollywood Hospice, therefore, maintains top clinicians and administrative staff, has an attractive facility, and recently attempted to make adjustments to apply for JCAHO (Joint Commission on Accreditation of Healthcare Organizations) accreditation. The administrative staff worked for several months revising policies and procedures and determining areas in which work practices should change to comply with JCAHO standards. The staff believed that improving standards for compliance would improve the quality of care of and bring prestige to the facility, even though it already has approval from the National Hospice Organization.

ORGANIZATIONAL PROBLEM

The administration of Hollywood Hospice knew that the changes were vital to achieving accreditation and had to be made quickly. The director, Ms. Cynthia Thurmond, distributed to each clinical and administrative department two-inch binders that contain details about the implementation procedures for accreditation. Shortly after distributing the binders and sending a reminder e-mail to all staff about the urgency of the implementation, Ms. Thurmond began to receive complaints from the administrative staff; the staff complained that most of the changes were not being followed by the clinicians. Ms. Thurmond expressed her frustrations to her assistant Glenn: "I don't understand why the clinicians aren't following the new protocols we gave them. Without full compliance with the new protocols, we have no chance for accreditation or for increased quality care."

"I know, but some of the changes are proving harder to implement than others; I'm not sure which ones we should have them focus on," Glenn responded. "I don't believe the clinicians understand that all of the new protocols have to be followed strictly.

Since 1951, The Joint Commission (JCAHO) has utilized profession-ally based standards as benchmarks for evaluating and accrediting health care organizations. Currently, JCAHO evaluates and accred-its over 18,000 health care organizations. Health care leaders and organizations recognize JCAHO accreditation as an indicator of qual-ity, based on compliance with performance standards. To maintain accreditation, health care organizations participate in a JCAHO sur-vey process about every three years.

The standards assess a health care organization's performance regarding adherence to its mission as well as processes that di-rectly affect patient care.

To prepare for the JCAHO survey process, JCAHO recommends that health care organizations take the following steps:

- Review the accreditation manual.
- Attend JCAHO and other seminars on the accreditation pro-cess.
- Contact other health care organizations that have completed the accreditation process.
- Identify the areas your organization does not meet compli-ance standards.
- Create a plan for improving areas that do not meet compli-ance standards.
- Educate clinical and administrative staff about the impor-tance and process of compliance.
- Engage in a mock survey.
- Address problems identified during the mock survey.
- Meet with clinical and administrative staff immediately prior to the JCAHO survey visit.

Source: Reprinted from Joint Commission on Accreditation of Healthcare Organizations' web site. "Facts About the Joint Com-mission on Accreditation of Healthcare Organizations." [Online in-formation; retrieval 2/17/98]. www.jcaho.org.

They just don't seem to care! Maybe we should create an incentive system so they'll do what we want," he suggested.

Meanwhile, down the hall, the medical director, Dr. George Frank, became very aggravated after reading the documents. "I can't believe they want us to make changes this quickly without giving our staff adequate training, and without even asking for our input!" he complained to a nurse. The nurse agreed, "All of these new policies and procedures are just more useless bureaucracy; who needs accreditation when we know we provide good quality healthcare? We have enough work as it is and we don't need more non-clinicians telling us what to do or how to do it."

Hollywood Hospice's compliance efforts appear to have reached a stalemate. Although its administration is ready to implement new policies and procedures for accreditation, the implementation lacks clinician support.

QUESTIONS FOR DISCUSSION

1. What areas display a communication break down? How could communication in these areas be improved?
2. Discuss how formalization plays a role in the scenario described in the case.
3. What could the administrative staff have done to better inform the clinical staff of the changes to be made for the accreditation process?
4. What could the administrative staff have done to prevent the negative response by the clinicians toward accreditation compliance?

PART TWO

Conflict and Negotiation

Case 3: Communicating Toward a Winning Team

☐ *Conflict and Negotiation*
◇ *Communication*
◎ *Specialty Clinic*

FOCUSED TOPIC DESCRIPTION

This case illustrates how proper team communication can help prevent conflict.

LEARNING/TEACHING OBJECTIVES

- To assess the potential benefits of using open communication to avoid conflicts among team members
- To assess how communication breakdowns can have a negative effect on an organization

BACKGROUND AND CASE OVERVIEW

The Southern Cystic Fibrosis Center (SCFC), located in Middleton, South Carolina, is one of the leading treatment and research centers for cystic fibrosis in the United States. Its success is due in part to its excellent staff and its overall organizational effectiveness. Its pediatric center is world renowned and boasts over 300 national and international annual patient visits.

Every Wednesday, a special clinic is held in the pediatric clinic on the main floor of a nearby tertiary care facility, Mercy Hospital. Dr. Robert Goodman, director of the pediatric program at Mercy, is a physician in the SCFC pediatric clinic. He works jointly with a multidisciplinary team of healthcare professionals to develop comprehensive care plans for patients and their families.

The staff of the SCFC decided that the best way to create overall health plans for patients and address issues concerning the clinic was to establish a care team, which would meet for about one hour every other Tuesday. The meeting was co-chaired by Dr. Goodman and Dr. Al Powers, a prominent pulmonologist. A social worker, dietitian, nurse coordinator, physical therapist, secretary, and pulmonary function technologist were also on the team.

During the initiation period of the care team, the team members were enthusiastic about coming together to improve the health of their patients. No one minded when meetings ran a little long or someone spoke out of turn because patients and care issues were being discussed and the team seemed to be accomplishing its goal of creating comprehensive and caring plans. In fact, the women on the care team often went to lunch together and socialized outside of the scheduled meetings.

ORGANIZATIONAL PROBLEM

The good times were soon to end. Problems began to arise about four months after the creation of the care team. The North American Cystic Fibrosis conference was on the agenda one summer afternoon. Dr. Goodman started the meeting by saying, "I wish that we had enough money to send all of you to the conference in Nashville, but the budget just doesn't look like its going to allow us to do that. Of course, Dr. Powers and myself, along with the other pulmonologists, will attend the meeting. That means we only have funds for four additional staff members to come along. The total cost per person is about $1,000, so it's unlikely that any of you will want to pay your own way. We need to decide who will benefit most from attending. Any suggestions on how to do this?"

Dr. Powers spoke up, "Well, I, for one, think that my secretary needs to attend. After all, she is responsible for a lot of the data entry and upkeep of our records. How much would a social worker and dietitian learn anyway? You would be bored out of your minds! You guys would be much better off staying behind. Besides, we need you here to manage the clinic."

From the irritated looks on their faces, the social worker and dietitian clearly did not appreciate Dr. Powers' belittling comment. Neither one said a word. The nurse coordinator spoke up in her defense, "I feel that my role as the head cystic fibrosis nurse should take precedence over a secretary. I resent the fact that you feel her work is more important than mine."

Dr. Powers immediately retorted with a snide remark, "Her dedication to her job makes her an automatic on the list so she will go. No more discussion on that subject is needed."

Reluctant to oppose his partner in the presence of the other committee members, Dr. Goodman said, "Three more spots left to fill." Immediately the nurse coordinator, social worker, dietitian, physical therapist, and pulmonary tech left the meeting room. Not a word was spoken as they left. Dr. Powers seemed unaffected by the discord he had just created and gloated that his personal secretary was one of the four staff members going to the meeting. Dr. Goodman expressed his disapproval by simply nodding his head and mumbling a few words about possibly finding extra money from pharmaceutical companies so the other staff members could go to the conference.

Over the next few weeks, the atmosphere of clinics became increasingly strained. Bitter e-mail messages that complained of favoritism and job dissatisfaction circulated among the five staff members who had walked out of the meeting, and they avoided Dr. Powers at all cost. The nurse coordinator and the physical therapist threatened to quit if they were not chosen to attend the conference, which angered the social worker, dietitian, and pulmonary tech because they thought that they were all sticking together as a team and supporting one another.

Dr. Goodman continued to raise funds to improve staff morale and keep them employed, but Dr. Powers's disrespectful demeanor and lack of appreciation became too much to bear for one staff member: The nurse coordinator quit three days after she threatened to do so.

QUESTIONS FOR DISCUSSION

1. What methods could have been used to improve decision making about the attendance at the National Cystic Fibrosis conference?
2. What were some of the communication break downs that brought about the rising conflict at the clinics?
3. Was the nurse coordinator justified in leaving the clinic? Did this act accomplish anything?

Case 4: Taking Care of Business at Graceland Memorial Hospital

☐ *Conflict and Negotiation*
◇ *Organizational Change*
○ *Hospital*

FOCUSED TOPIC DESCRIPTION

This case proves that regulatory changes have a significant effect on healthcare organizations and can cause conflict as an organization adapts to them.

LEARNING/TEACHING OBJECTIVES

- To encourage students to evaluate both sides of a conflict
- To use theory when developing alternatives for responding to organizational change

BACKGROUND AND CASE OVERVIEW

Graceland Memorial Hospital is a not-for-profit, community hospital located in a medium-sized urban area in the Midwest. The only other hospital that serves this community is a large, tertiary care teaching hospital affiliated with a major university medical center.

When Jack Prestwood, vice president of Human Resources at Graceland, read the current Occupational Safety and Health Administration (OSHA) regulations, he knew that he needed to comply with them. Under the newly formed OSHA regulations, Graceland is required to enforce the correct usage of respiratory masks and conduct respiratory fit-testing to prevent the transmission of communicable diseases. In the past, Graceland employees who had frequent contact with patients who suffered from airborne communicable diseases were not fitted for a correctly sized respiratory mask. Therefore, to prevent large OSHA fines for noncompliance with the new regulations, Graceland's administration concluded that it must update its own regulations.

ORGANIZATIONAL PROBLEM

Mr. Prestwood called Janet Bowers, director of Employee Health, into his office one morning to ask, "Janet, are you familiar with the new OSHA regulations for respiratory mask fit-testing?"

"I certainly am, Jack," replied Ms. Bowers. "After reading about the OSHA update in *Employee Health Weekly*, I called our two health equipment supply companies yesterday afternoon to get an idea of the costs involved with mask fit-testing. I knew that I would need the information sooner or later since the hospital will obviously have to comply with the new regulations."

"Sounds great, Janet. What did you find out?" asked Mr. Prestwood.

"It seems that both companies will give us a discount for a large order of the masks. They will also provide training to Employee Health and Infection Control staffs for proper use of the new masks, " Ms. Bowers continued.

"It looks like you've done your homework, Janet. Let's schedule a meeting with the Infection Control staff about this," Mr. Prestwood suggested.

Mr. Prestwood arranged the meeting the next day with Ms. Bowers and Erika Thompson, the director of Infection Control, to discuss the updated OSHA regulations and the proposed compliance change. To Mr. Prestwood and Ms. Bowers' surprise, Ms. Thompson objected to implementing the change.

"Why should we have to undergo such a major policy change since the other hospitals in the area are not making any changes in their infection control policies?" Ms. Thompson complained. "That's only going to require more work for my staff and for me. I really don't think that the change is worth the cost of its implementation. I recommend that we keep things as they are. The current policies have worked just fine for the past couple of years. If other hospitals begin to make the change, then maybe we could decide to update our policies."

After the meeting with Ms. Thompson, Mr. Prestwood was very frustrated. As a vice president, he had a legal and moral obligation to implement changes for compliance. Although few hospitals had begun to implement the new safety measures within their Infection Control departments, he was concerned about the potential risk of following in their footsteps. Graceland had always been known as a leader but now he was thinking of dragging behind with the pack. But there could be fines to pay; after all, the new guidelines were the law, and if there was an accident, the consequences could be worse! He did not understand why Ms. Thompson's response to the situation was different from others in the past.

To find a solution to the dispute, Mr. Prestwood arranged another meeting with Ms. Bowers and Ms. Thompson, but this time he also invited Margaret Ridell, vice president of Medical Staff Affairs, and two doctors on the medical staff. All, except for

The Occupational Safety and Health Administration (OSHA) was established to prevent workplace injuries and protect the health of America's more than 100 million workers covered by the Occupational Safety and Health Act of 1970. The majority of working men and women—including health professionals—fall under OSHA's jurisdiction.

Specifically, the Occupational Safety and Health Act of 1970 was passed "to assure safe and healthful working conditions for working men and women; by authorizing enforcement of the standards developed under the Act; by assisting and encouraging the States in their efforts to assure safe and healthful working conditions; by providing for research, information, education, and training in the field of occupational safety and health; and for other purposes."

The primary activity of OSHA is workplace inspections. OSHA and its state partners have a diverse staff of professionals, including 2,100 inspectors, located in more than 200 offices throughout the country. These professionals develop and enforce standards to protect employees as well as provide technical assistance and consultation to employers and employees.

Source: Reprinted from Occupational Safety and Health Administration web site. "Information About OSHA" and "OSHA Act of 1970." [Online information; retrieval 3/30/98]. www.osha.gov.

Ms. Thompson, agreed with Mr. Prestwood's recommendation. Ms. Thompson, who represents the aggregate view of Infection Control, still would not voice her support for the policy change. After two hours of intense discussion, no clear resolution had been reached. Mr. Prestwood decided that he would have to look at other avenues by which to get the new fit-testing requirement in place.

QUESTIONS FOR DISCUSSION

1. What are the opposing perspectives presented in this case? Are there deeper issues involved than those on the surface? Do you agree with either side? Why?
2. Why might Infection Control be resistant to this change?
3. If Mr. Prestwood were to implement this policy change, to which internal and external resources might he turn for support?
4. Assuming that fit-testing was implemented, would you anticipate resistance from employees? If so, how would you overcome it?

PART THREE

Customers and the Environment

Case 5: Stop the Presses!

☐ *Customers and the Environmental Domain*
◇ *Environment*
◎ *Hospital*

FOCUSED TOPIC DESCRIPTION

This case features the administration of a government hospital that is faced with the dilemma of addressing publicly voiced complaints about the quality and delivery of its care.

LEARNING/TEACHING OBJECTIVES

- To examine how to manage negative public relations concerning patient quality of care and delivery issues
- To learn the importance of trust between a health service organization and the community it serves

BACKGROUND AND CASE OVERVIEW

Pima Indian Hospital (PIH) is a hospital that serves Native Americans of the Pima tribe of Arizona. PIH operates under the aegis of the Indian Health Service (IHS), which is subordinate to the U.S. Department of Health and Human Services.

27

The 32-bed hospital provides healthcare services to eligible Native Americans at no cost. The hospital was founded in the late 1950s and has been housed in two separate locations since. Throughout its history, there have been recurrent conflicts between the tribe and the IHS over how the hospital should be operated. Many of the executives within PIH are people with political connections with the tribe. Although these executives appeared to meet minimum qualifications, there may have been more well-qualified applicants who lacked connections. As a result of these hiring practices and conflicts, PIH has constantly been under fire from genuinely dissatisfied patients and critics whose aim is to discredit the IHS. The tribe has conducted many studies to determine whether it should assume PIH's operations; the results of these studies have been equivocal.

Over the past few years, sentiments against PIH have risen dramatically. PIH could not retain top health administrators for extended periods. The executives who used to hold the medical director and Health Services administrator positions have found dealing with the tribe's leadership—the tribal council and chief—extremely difficult. The tribal leadership has been pushing for exclusive tribal operation of the hospital. However, their purported takeover bid has been viewed with cynicism by those who work at the hospital. Community members seem equally split on the issue—some side with the tribe while others align with PIH.

ORGANIZATIONAL PROBLEM

The tension finally came to a head. A group of tribal members sent an editorial regarding the poor quality of care at PIH to the *Phoenix Sun*, the major daily newspaper in Phoenix, Arizona. The newspaper, in turn, sent reporters to interview the authors of the editorial about their opinion on the state of affairs at PIH. In their haste to complete the story, the reporters did not pursue an interview with either the PIH administrator or medical director. Over five days, the *Phoenix Sun* published a series of articles on PIH based solely on the tribe's point of view; the first article made the front page.

The recent events and highly publicized accusations had obviously disturbed many staff members. Anxiety among staff was high as they assembled for the monthly hospital-wide meeting: the providers and support staff gathered in small groups talking among themselves. The actual Health Services administrator was attending a month-long patient care workshop in Washington, D.C., so Mr. Nash, the acting administrator, presided over the meeting.

Before the meeting, Mr. Nash anxiously gazed over the crowd, looking for cues that would help him choose the tone of his delivery. He opened the meeting by introducing himself and telling the staff that he was only at PIH temporarily, then he turned the meeting over to Mr. Bradford, head of the Health Promotion division, to introduce the interns who were working at the hospital for the summer, which was a good non-issue with which to introduce a potentially inflammatory meeting. The employees were beginning to grow restless as the moments wore on because their frustrations were not being immediately addressed. Sensing this underlying tension, Mr. Nash wisely took back the charge of the discussion.

"I know everyone here is familiar with the newspaper reports of the past few days and are rightly concerned about these statements and accusations. These reports charge that the quality of care at PIH is being compromised by poor administrative decisions and inadequately trained staff," Mr. Nash summarized.

"How can people accuse us of making poor decisions when the tribe is constantly interfering with the administration of the hospital? Also, what do they mean by inadequacy? I have been here for 20 years and I know that the physicians and medical staff are highly trained and are extremely dedicated to serving Native Americans," Dr. Bulwhark, a physician at PIH, interrupted.

"I know there have been some physicians who have worked here who were not that great, but they are no longer here. I believe that we should respond to these complaints with our own analysis of the situation. If we don't, the public will believe the stories that they read in the papers. If we don't defend our position, they will believe that we acknowledge these allegations as true. We should act as soon as possible to uphold our integrity," he concluded.

"I agree with you, Dr. Bulwhark. These allegations can be very damaging to our credibility as a healthcare provider," Mr. Nash replied nervously. "However, in order to publicly respond to these claims, we must go through the chain of command to obtain approval. Since the administrator is not here, I am the first in the chain of command. But we'll have to go through the area director, then he has to go through the head of IHS who, in turn, has to go to the head of the Department of Health and Human Services. This will take an inordinate amount of time to complete. I'm afraid by the time we get approval, the time to effectively respond will have expired. Thus, we'll have to hold our tongues for the duration of these incidents," Mr. Nash explained.

The crowd seemed shocked by this response; some asked questions about how the hospital could respond appropriately. Mr. Nash again repeated the procedure on issuing an official response to public allegations. The staff, seeing that no course of action was proposed, was visibly angry. Mr. Nash quickly summed up the meeting and retreated to his office.

Spurred by the exposé of the newspaper articles, the conflict did not subside but continued to grow. The sentiments of the tribal council reflected the concerns of its members, and the tribal council once again started to investigate proceedings on the feasibility of taking over the operations of PIH. Two months after the newspaper reports broke, the Health Services administrator and medical director resigned. In addition, the pharmacy of the hospital became understaffed after three pharmacists resigned and it could not immediately recruit replacement personnel.

PIH appeared to be falling apart. PIH's critics responded by urging the tribe to file a lawsuit against the hospital for failure to provide adequate health services. The tribe agreed and began proceedings against PIH.

QUESTIONS FOR DISCUSSION

1. What was the dilemma at Pima Indian Hospital (PIH)? What are some of its causes?
2. Identify all of the stakeholders in this conflict. Which ones appear to wield the most power?
3. How could the administration handle this problem effectively? What could Mr. Nash have said differently at the staff meeting to generate positive feedback on addressing the problem?
4. Suppose that several members of the medical staff decided to submit a joint editorial to the *Phoenix Sun* that responded to many of the issues brought forth by the critics. How would the administration react to this development?

Case 6: The Rocky Road to Patient Satisfaction at Leonard-Griggs

☐ *Customers and the Environmental Domain*
◇ *Organizational Structure: Formalization*
◎ *Management Service Organization*

FOCUSED TOPIC DESCRIPTION

This case argues that employees must be satisfied in their respective jobs to provide the highest standard of care and fulfill
the desires of the patient population.

LEARNING/TEACHING OBJECTIVES

- To recognize the importance of revising job descriptions
  when employee responsibility is increased and additional tasks are assigned
- To develop an understanding of how ineffective communication can create bitterness and misunderstanding
- To assess the need for and the significance of patient
  satisfaction survey data in a rural healthcare setting

BACKGROUND AND CASE INFORMATION

Leonard-Griggs Primary Care System is a network of physician practices located in rural South Carolina. The network presently includes five sites. Three of the sites, including the parent site and the two larger satellite clinics, are located in Haycock County. These sites are well established and have positive relationships with the community. The other two satellite clinics, located in separate adjoining counties, have been recently acquired by Leonard-Griggs. Neither county has any major metropolitan areas. The communities of these counties are traditionally underserved, change comes less easily for them, and their satellite clinics have had some difficulty establishing themselves and marketing their services among this very dispersed population. The satellite clinics are no more than 20 miles from the main clinic and administrative office.

Leonard-Griggs's mission is to provide comprehensive, quality primary and preventive healthcare services to all citizens of the region, regardless of the patient's financial or insurance status. Leonard-Griggs is important to the community because it is committed to serving everyone regardless of one's ability to pay. By providing primary healthcare services to the "unassigned" or underinsured patients in the area, Leonard-Griggs supports the medical staff, enhances physician retention and recruitment efforts, and reduces the overall healthcare costs for the community. To maintain the current patient base and attract new patients to sustain revenue, Leonard-Griggs must continue to perfect its patient focus and service per requests of the patients.

ORGANIZATIONAL PROBLEM

Leonard-Griggs employs 12 providers and a support staff of approximately 60 individuals including nurses, certified nursing assistants, clerical support staff, and billing personnel. The majority of the employees, particularly those who assist in the individual physician offices, have worked for Leonard-Griggs since its opening. The responsibilities of these employees, as well as various other staff members, generally do not differ greatly from day to day.

To try to better serve patients, Sadie Ratcliff, the executive director, decided to implement a patient satisfaction effort at each of the five physician practices. Key to the effort would be the ongoing collection of data using a survey instrument. The surveys would reveal patient opinions of services, office staff, nursing staff, providers, and geographic location of the site. Ms. Ratcliff informed each of the administrative managers of her intentions at the weekly meeting and enlisted the assistance of the summer intern, Jessie Hartley, in starting the project. The manager of Human Resources was especially supportive of the surveys: "These surveys will reveal any possible changes in personnel I should make and will show just where our system's focus should be." Jessie was assigned to deliver the surveys, along with incentives for patients to complete the surveys, to all five sites. The incentive is that each patient would receive a gift—a notepad with the network logo and site-specific information—at checkout for agreeing to complete the survey there or take it home.

On Monday morning, Jessie walked into Shady Bluff Medical Clinic, the first site to receive the surveys. She began to explain the plan of action to Ms. Robin, the employee responsible for checkout procedures—collecting payments at the time of patient departure and scheduling return appointments. Ms. Robin has worked for Shady Bluff since it opened 17 years ago, so she has established a particular way to perform every aspect of her job and perform them quite naturally. Although the people she has met since Leonard-Griggs purchased Shady Bluff seemed like good people, she still was not sure about their new methods, including distributing the patient satisfaction survey.

"I'm not sure I can remember to give out the surveys as patients come to my window to check out," Ms. Robin explained to Jessie. "Why should I have to take the time to explain the survey format to patients, especially those who are ill, and give out notepads? I just can't do all of my work and this work, too!"

"Ms. Robin, please do the best you can," Jessie cautiously replied. "If you miss a few patients, no big deal. Just try to hand the surveys to patients as often as you can and stress the importance of responses. Management feels patient satisfaction surveys are tools that can lead to a more efficient, patient-friendly organization and I'm sure your efforts will be appreciated."

As Jessie walked out the front door of the office, Ms. Robin placed the boxes of surveys and notepads under the counter. "Well, it appears that Ms. Ratcliff does not feel obligated to personally speak with office staff about the issue," Ms. Robin thought. "The instructions Jessie gave me are so vague, so I see no reason to go out of my way to tell patients to complete them. Besides, I'm tired of handling duties that are not included in my job description. These additional tasks involve just enough work to make my day even more hectic."

Jessie continued to deliver the surveys and gift notepads to the remaining four sites. At each clinic, office personnel were surprised at the new procedure that took effect right away. Mrs. Lorene, an employee at the Oak Grove site, offered her concerns: "Many of our regular patients cannot read and some can't write. Can relatives or friends complete the surveys? What about children who come in for check-ups and are too young to speak for themselves? These things are more trouble than they are worth."

While driving back to the administrative office, Jessie was confused and discouraged. She wondered why Ms. Ratcliff had not mentioned the survey implementation process to employees at last month's staff meeting. Certainly, Jessie thought to herself, patients could sense tension in the attitudes and actions of the support staff, which could create a negative perception of the office visit and, therefore, result in negative responses on the survey.

Jessie and Ms. Ratcliff met for an hour the same afternoon. Jessie relayed the responses of the office employees and her own concerns: "I feel caught in the middle and the employees are not willing to listen to me. I think an administrator probably needs to provide guidance. I don't want to be thought of as a know it all."

Ms. Ratcliff gave her a few suggestions for responding to the complaints and promised to send a memo to "get everyone on board with this endeavor." Jessie was somewhat encouraged, but still feared overstepping her boundaries. She wanted to tell Ms. Ratcliff that confusion and low employee morale seemed to be two deterrents to the success of the implementation, but she was not sure whether or not she should share her opinions because she was only an intern.

Many procedural questions were left unanswered, including what to do with the surveys as they came back to the clinics and whether patients could receive more than one survey given that most of them returned for rechecks. Jessie realized that making employees feel like team players would help them accept increased job responsibility with enthusiasm. A plan for turning the patient satisfaction survey crisis around needed prompt consideration.

QUESTIONS FOR DISCUSSION

1. How does Leonard-Griggs's degree of centralization affect the problem of disgruntled employees? Would a lower or higher degree of centralization improve the situation?
2. What could Ms. Ratcliff do to better prepare employees for new responsibilities?

3. If the tasks performed by the majority of the employees are routine, then what reasons do they have for shunning the implementation of the patient satisfaction surveys? In your opinion, should the job description of checkout employees be revised to include this task?
4. Explain reasons for Jessie's anxiety over instructing employees. What could have better prepared her for the assignment?

PART FOUR

Decision Making

Case 7: The Ax Man Cometh

☐ *Decision Making*
◇ *Organizational Change*
◯ *Hospital*

FOCUSED TOPIC DESCRIPTION

This case presents a senior management dilemma—how to facilitate group decision making on presenting to employees the downsizing of a senior executive.

LEARNING/TEACHING OBJECTIVES

- To highlight the importance of processes and outcomes of group decision making for managers of hospitals and other healthcare organizations
- To apply group decision-making processes and increase awareness of group decision-making errors

BACKGROUND AND CASE OVERVIEW

Lenoa Hospital is located in a rural college town in the western part of the country. It has enjoyed a reputation for quality care and financial stability for over 80 years. Until recently, it has been spared the wave of managed care in the region. Two integrated health systems in the state capital have been expanding and moving into Lenoa's market area. The effect of this expansion is starting to show on Lenoa's bottom line via contracts lost and declining revenues.

ORGANIZATIONAL PROBLEM

"I say we do it all now and get it over with. Why prolong the anxiety among the employees?"

The subject is the announcement of the elimination of a senior management staff; the speaker is the newly hired chief operating officer (COO), Bruce Oldham; the scene is a retreat of the senior management group. The senior management group, composed of seven members, had made some very difficult decisions over the course of the previous two days: it eliminated 18 positions, including George Mason's, and four small departments of this community-owned, not-for-profit hospital. The group anticipated that employees would be particularly upset by the elimination of Mr. Mason, a senior executive who had been with Lenoa for 25 years.

"Mr. Mason's 25 years of service to this facility should be worth some special treatment," argued aloud the director of Human Resources, Jane Miranda, but her inner voice said, "Great! Eighty years of providing quality healthcare without a single layoff and now I get to be the lucky person responsible for coordinating this one percent downsize of our workforce."

The era of managed care had finally caught up with Lenoa and its effect was not pretty. Lenoa was not in bad shape financially—not yet, anyway—but it had some catching up to do and fast. Larger health systems based in the state capital, located 85 miles away, were beginning to infringe upon Lenoa's market area and the effects were starting to be seen. Benchmark analysis showed expenses that were far too high for a 208-bed hospital that offers its service mix.

The retreat's sole purpose was to derive a solution to effectively reduce salary expenditures and save money without minimizing the quality of patient care. However, the senior management group seemed stuck. "Groupthink" seemed to have weakened the group's creative decision-making skills.

"This is a decision we have to make this afternoon. The other eliminated positions are going to be announced at the department manager's meeting in less than a week. Is that when we're going to announce that George's position has been eliminated?" Mr. Oldham continued. "If we string this process out for too long, we're going to have a hospital full of anxious employees wondering if they're next."

"Then you really will live up to your reputation as 'the ax man'," Mrs. Miranda remarked. "I think employees are going to be anxious no matter how we do it. Mr. Mason deserves a separate announcement. I don't want to have his name on the same memo as that of a food service employee with only two years of service."

QUESTIONS FOR DISCUSSION

1. Name and describe the potential decision-making errors that this senior management group could make, which could reduce the quality of their decision.
2. Notice the dialogue in this case. What steps could Mr. Oldham take to avoid groupthink?
3. How could the meeting be structured to overcome potential group decision-making errors?
4. Suppose that the group decides to announce the elimination of Mr. Mason at the same time that the rest of the cuts are announced. What are the potential

negative organizational behavior outcomes? Are there potential positive organizational behavior outcomes that ought to be considered as well? Should the group give consideration to Mr. Mason's probable personal reaction?

Case 8: To Have or Not to Have Centralized Scheduling

☐ *Decision Making*
◇ *Organizational Structure: Centralization*
◯ *Hospital*

FOCUSED TOPIC DESCRIPTION

This case supports that the amount of control senior management has in making decisions within the organization is related to the degree of centralization within an organization.

LEARNING/TEACHING OBJECTIVES

- To learn the relationship between centralization and decentralization and the degree of control that senior managers have in making decisions
- To determine the effects of centrally made decisions in a decentralized and largely horizontally differentiated structure
- To explore alternative ways to make decisions in a decentralized organization

BACKGROUND AND CASE OVERVIEW

Centraltown Medical Center (CMC) is a public, not-for-profit, teaching medical center located in West Haven, California, and is affiliated with a major public university, Centraltown University. CMC has 665 beds in its General Hospital, Burn Center, Clinical Cancer Center, Women's and Children's Hospital, and Neurosciences Hospital. Approximately 25,000 patients are admitted each year and over 500,000 outpatients are seen annually in the main hospital, as well as at the Ambulatory Care Center (ACC), at the Family Practice Center, and in the multiple satellite clinics. CMC strives to provide high quality healthcare to the people of West Haven and its surrounding communities and supports medical education for healthcare professionals. Numerous private and group practices, urgent care centers, ambulatory centers, home health agencies, and nursing homes are located in and around the West Haven area.

Only 15 miles away from CMC is Benton University Medical Center (BUMC), a prestigious and world renowned teaching, research, and medical facility associated with Benton University. BUMC is a private, not-for-profit 1,124-bed hospital with close to 35,000 inpatient admissions and 700,325 outpatient visits.

Because of the nature and the size of CMC, its structure is decentralized with high horizontal differentiation. Clinical departments within the hospital are relatively undifferentiated horizontally, with the director of each division reporting directly to the hospital's chief operating officer. Only a few physician directors and administrative directors, as well as the chief of staff and the CEO, supervise the departments and clinics within the hospital. Because the business of CMC is healthcare, the physicians and administrators generally share in power and decision making because they depend on one another to successfully run the hospital.

During the last five years, CMC and BUMC have grown increasingly competitive as managed care moved rapidly to establish itself in the state. The hospitals are continually competing for contracts and patients, but as healthcare prices continue to fall, the two hospitals have had to find alternative and unique ways to secure new patients and managed care contracts. With outpatient services growing in demand, the hospitals have especially concentrated on innovative ways to improve these services.

ORGANIZATIONAL PROBLEM

In a recent departmental director's meeting, the CEO, Ed Holton, came to speak to the physician directors about centralized scheduling. He explained what centralized scheduling was, how a central scheduling system would work at CMC, and what the benefits would be. He then announced that he and his administrative committee had decided to integrate the scheduling at CMC and that the hospital would be operating under a centralized scheduling system within the next seven months.

Many of the physicians present during the meeting were upset by the news and disagreed aloud with Mr. Holton. Others questioned his assumptions. The physicians argued that a centralized scheduling system would (1) be too costly to implement immediately and (2) cause them to lose even more control and freedom within the healthcare arena. In addition, the physicians claimed that assuming that one system could fit the scheduling needs of every clinic and department within BUMC is preposterous. Several physicians suggested that the system should be tested on a small scale first. Mr. Holton, angered that his presentation had not been positively received, refused to listen to the physicians' suggestions and alternatives. The meeting ended when Mr. Holton stormed out of the room after the chief of staff, Dr. Raysha Naile, suggested that a committee, composed of both administrators and physicians, be created to look into centralized scheduling and other alternative scheduling systems.

Three days later, Dr. Naile made an appointment to see Mr. Holton to talk about the incident and to come up with a solution to the problem. The following dialogue transpired.

Dr. Naile: Thank you for seeing me. As you probably know, I would like to talk about the last meeting. I think that your idea for CMC to adopt a centralized scheduling system is an excellent idea. In fact, I believe that it is necessary for CMC to change the way appointments are made because right now patients are calling over a hundred different phone numbers just to make an appointment for an outpatient procedure or visit.

Mr. Holton: Then why did you contradict me in front of all of the departmental directors? That was humiliating and defiant!

Dr. Naile: I was not disagreeing with you. I merely suggested that a committee should be formed to discuss and decide on the best method for everyone. I think that the physicians were a little taken aback when, without consultation, they were told that a new system that would completely change clinics' operations was to be implemented. I think that they have a right to participate in the decision making that affects CMC clinics.

Mr. Holton: I'm the CEO here! Not you and not the physicians! I'm the one who makes decisions about this hospital. I know what's right for it. CMC needs a way to better satisfy its patients. If the physicians can't see this, then they will have to just live with my choice anyway. Besides, I have a committee and we've decided centralized scheduling was the best alternative.

Dr. Naile: Ed, I'm on your side! I agree that CMC needs an alternative way to schedule patients, but I think that centralized scheduling is a major change. It cannot happen overnight. We need....

Mr. Holton: Yes it can. I've met with the clinic managers and the administrators. They agree that centralized scheduling is necessary to secure patients in the future.

Dr. Naile: As I already said, I agree. But we need the support of the physicians for this project.

Mr. Holton: I'm sorry, Dr. Naile, but you don't understand. This isn't something to be negotiated. As CEO, I determined that a scheduling problem existed, my committee and I researched the problem and looked for solutions, and I chose the best alternative for CMC. Now if you'll excuse me, I'm presenting this to the board in five minutes.

The board of directors passed the motion to adopt a centralized scheduling system. At the time of the vote, they were unaware of any disagreement over the issue. The board also created a steering committee to plan and implement centralized scheduling. Based on Mr. Holton's suggestions, the committee was composed of three clinic managers, an accountant, the associate director of Finance, the chief operating officer, a statistician, a registered nurse, and one physician.

A month later, the Implementation Committee began contacting the physician directors of each clinic to obtain the information necessary to create scheduling manuals. To begin creating a single scheduling program, the committee needed such information as the average time each type of visit and procedure took, the rooms and equipment used in each type of visit, and authorizations needed before scheduling a visit. However, many of the physicians refused to provide the necessary information.

Throughout the years, the clinics had become independent from one another in the way patients were scheduled and visits were conducted. Many appointments were scheduled by the physicians' personal secretaries, other appointments were scheduled in the business offices of the physicians' departments, and the remaining appointments were scheduled by the front desk personnel in the clinics. Without proper cooperation from the physicians, the committee would need several additional months to determine what procedures needed x-rays, blood sampling, or other tests; to find out which types of visits needed authorizations or referrals first; and to ascertain what pieces of equipment or special rooms were required for certain visits. The committee was forced to hire a consulting firm at an added expense to the hospital of $500,000. The consulting firm spent two months just determining all of the clinical information necessary to schedule appointments for each clinic.

The medical staff scorned the entire process, and CMC became divided on a number of issues after the centralized scheduling fiasco. Many physicians were so disgusted by the way the issue was handled that they left CMC to practice at BUMC and other facilities. The hospital lost hundreds of thousands of dollars. Eventually, Mr. Holton resigned from his position. The new CEO spent over eight months focusing on methods to improve the poor relationship between physicians and administrators, rather than on researching new ways to win over patients to CMC.

QUESTIONS FOR DISCUSSION

1. Why did Mr. Holton believe that it was unnecessary for the physicians to participate in the decision making? Why did the physicians want to be involved in the decision-making process?
2. What alternative methods could Mr. Holton have used in the decision-making process?
3. What changes should the new CEO enact to prevent a similar situation from happening again?

PART FIVE

External Environment

Case 9: Declining Census and Its Effects on Motivation and Morale

☐ *Environment*
◇ *Motivation*
◎ *Rehabilitation Center*

FOCUSED TOPIC DESCRIPTION

This case focuses on the effect of the external environment on employee morale.

LEARNING/TEACHING OBJECTIVES

- To learn about environmental scanning
- To explore methods for improving employee morale

BACKGROUND AND CASE OVERVIEW

Scarecrow Rehabilitation Center (SRC) is a 105-bed, brain injury rehabilitation healthcare facility located in Midville, Pennsylvania. As a pioneer in its field, SRC is one of four American facilities that specializes solely in brain injury rehabilitation; it is the only such facility located in the Northeast. SRC is a freestanding, private, for-profit organization that is accredited by JCAHO. Its mission is to provide the highest quality patient care, treatment, and education, and conduct research in the most cost-effective manner.

Because of its outstanding reputation and innovative services, SRC has received national and international referrals for the past ten years. Its cutting-edge technologies surpassed those of other rehabilitation centers in the Northeast. Until recently, SRC operated at full capacity, with a 100 percent bed occupancy rate. The patient census mix was approximately 85 percent commercial payers and 15 to 20 percent Medicare and other payer sources.

ORGANIZATIONAL PROBLEM

SRC experienced an unexpected downturn in its patient census during the past six months. The patient census was averaging only 85 patients and the percent of commercial–payer patients was declining. The executive administration became quite concerned about this trend and charged the Marketing/Admissions department with conducting an investigation.

Marketing/Admissions identified multiple external factors that were influencing the incidence of brain injury-related accidents. Nearby states and Canadian provinces were requiring drivers to wear seatbelts. Almost all states, with the exception of Ohio, required motorcyclists to wear helmets. There was an increasing usage of bicycle helmets among small children and adolescents in response to the federal government's campaign that advocated for bicycle safety. Marketing/Admissions also discovered that air bags had greatly reduced severe traumatic head injury but had increased the need for mild acute head injury monitoring.

Marketing/Admissions concluded the decreasing census was also related to the increasing number of rehabilitation facilities that expand their product lines to include a brain trauma center.

The number of brain trauma centers in the United States had increased by over 100 percent, with a total of 10 facilities located throughout the country. Two of the new facilities were located in the Northeast, including a facility just 100 miles away in Youngstown, Ohio. In addition, many hospitals were beginning to offer brain injury services as part of their continuum of care. For example, the American Medical Association recently recognized the University of Pittsburgh for outstanding achievement in neurosurgery.

In response to the decreasing patient census, the SRC administration directed Marketing/Admissions to increase census to the previous level, or staff would have to be laid off. Traditionally, Marketing/Admissions was a highly cohesive, motivated, goal-oriented professional staff. However, given the magnitude of the problem and the seemingly unrealistic expectations now placed on them, the staff began to display signs of increased anxiety and decreased morale.

The director of Marketing/Admissions, Jennifer Hines, called a meeting of her staff. "What's going on here?" she asked. "Why is our admission rate plummeting?"

"It's simple," an employee replied. "No one here anticipated that there would ever be competition in the field of brain injury rehabilitation. Whose job is that anyway?"

"Do you know where the layoffs will begin? Is it based on tenure?" another employee questioned. "Thank goodness I've been here for five years!"

"What?" countered another employee. "I know I haven't been here too long, but I need this job and no one else here has the skills or knowledge that I have!"

The atmosphere of the meeting became increasingly hostile as each employee argued why he or she should not be laid off. The committee never addressed the issue of how SRC could attract more patients.

QUESTIONS FOR DISCUSSION

1. What preventive measures could Scarecrow Rehabili-
    tation Center (SRC) have taken to avoid the present
    situation?
2. What suggestions would you provide to Ms. Hines to
    address the current problems?
3. Identify techniques SRC management could use to
    improve employee morale.

Case 10: Strategies for Serving an Atypical Patient Population

☐ *Environment*
◇ *Organizational Culture*
◎ *Migrant Health Network*

FOCUSED TOPIC DESCRIPTION

This case explores the role of an organization in a turbulent external environment and how to meet the needs of a hard-to-reach migrant population.

LEARNING/TEACHING OBJECTIVES

- To identify organizational strategies for working effectively in a changing environment
- To explore the challenges of working with unique patient populations such as migrant farmworkers

BACKGROUND AND CASE OVERVIEW

Healthy Farmworkers (HF) is a not-for-profit organization that places outreach workers in areas along the East Coast of the United States. Areas are selected for a high concentration of migrant farmworkers, particularly Hispanic migrant farmworkers. These areas are typically rural communities with a high density of farms and packing houses. Outreach workers are selected based on several criteria including bilingual ability; competence to coordinate with different organizations such as churches, health departments, rural health centers, rural physicians, and farms; and a desire to help people in need. The main duties of outreach workers, which also represent the mission of the organization, are to educate farmworkers on health issues, promote health awareness, and provide medical services.

The major challenge in helping migrant farmworkers is developing trust between the farmworker and the outreach worker. Developing this trust is the key to encouraging farmworkers to become receptive to outside help, especially help related to gaining access to better healthcare services. Also, once a trust-based relationship is established, the farmworkers are more likely to assist the outreach worker in reaching other farmworkers in the community and locating other migrant camps. Unfortunately, changing immigration laws and increased Immigration and Naturalization Service (INS) surveillance makes building such relationships more difficult. Given the changes in the external environment, it is increasingly difficult to assure illegal migrant farmworkers that social security numbers and documents are not needed for medical treatment.

ORGANIZATIONAL PROBLEM

Juan Martinez, an illegal migrant farmworker, who speaks no English and is anxious because of recent INS raids in the area, remarks to the outreach worker in Spanish: "I do not go to the health center because they always ask for pay stubs, a social security number, my local home address, and telephone number. I am scared that someone will use the information to track me down and deport me. I paid a lot of money to get here. I do not want to go back."

One of Juan's friends, Oscar Ramos, comments: "I do not like to go to the doctors because they don't speak Spanish and they charge me so much money. I do not feel comfortable there and I feel as if I am not wanted there. Those doctors make me do all this paperwork which I cannot fill out. It makes me very uncomfortable."

Excuses for not seeking medical treatment are common among migrant farmworkers. Outreach workers must be able to overcome farmworkers' fears to be successful in increasing access to health services for this population.

The local health department has increasingly found itself in a dilemma. It has a mandate to serve the health needs of its population, but because of the changing external environment, migrants are leery of working with any formal organization. While the health department has mounted various outreach programs to various populations, its dominant practice is to expect patients to seek out services at the health department. Also, the health department employees believe that they are overworked with the people who come to the clinic, so responding to the challenge of creating more outreach programs is too overwhelming.

Given the health department's conflict, the efforts of HF are critical to improving the health of migrants. HF outreach workers often seek out community leaders to help serve migrant farmworkers, especially when the outreach workers are working in multiple communities. Thus, outreach workers try to develop long-term solutions to coordinate care for the farmworkers. A plan for continuous care of the migrant farmworkers must take into account the ever increasing and continuously changing migrant population. Although farmworkers may return each year to pick crops, the same outreach workers may not be in a community from year to year.

QUESTIONS FOR DISCUSSION

1. What justification(s) exist(s) for the health department to develop a strategy for addressing the healthcare needs of migrant farmworkers?
2. How could the outreach worker alleviate fears that Hispanic migrant workers have about government organizations, including the health department? How could the outreach worker convince them to use the health services?
3. How can the outreach workers help the health department staff in thinking of a creative response to the unsettled legal environment of migrant farmworkers?
4. What type of long-term plans could be developed to provide continuous medical service to the migrants from year to year?
5. How can an outreach worker develop trust with the migrant workers?

Case 11: Patient Satisfaction Up In Smoke

☐ *Environment*
◇ *Customers and the Environmental Domain*
◎ *Hospital*

FOCUSED TOPIC DESCRIPTION

This case illustrates how an organization's environment may negatively affect patient satisfaction.

LEARNING/TEACHING OBJECTIVES

- To understand how the environment of an organization can affect patient satisfaction
- To examine how accreditation processes can lead to improvements in patient satisfaction

BACKGROUND AND CASE OVERVIEW

Smith Regional Medical Center (SRMC) is located in Smith County, Missouri. SRMC is a 238-bed, not-for-profit, community hospital. Its mission is to improve the health status of Smith

County—a mid-sized community of about 30,000 people—and its surrounding communities. SRMC is set geographically between three major competitors, two of which are academic medical centers and the third is a large community hospital; all three competitors are located approximately 30 miles from SRMC. In comparison, SRMC is smaller than the three hospitals and does not provide as many specialized services.

Hospital administrators have always believed that the environment of the hospital is a key determinant in making patients and visitors feel welcome and well cared for during their visit. Therefore, SRMC was built with an architectural design that alluded to the hospital's innovation, technology, and commitment to patient satisfaction. The interior was designed to express professionalism and exude warmth to enhance patient comfort and satisfaction. In addition, the building was structured to make it easy for patients to find their destination.

However, smoking at patient entrances, by patients, visitors, and employees, has been a problem at SRMC since its opening. The entrances into the hospital are often a patient's first impression of the facility; smoking at the entrances completely undermines the intent of the hospital design.

ORGANIZATIONAL PROBLEM

Recently, smoking at patient entrances has become unbearable for people who enter the hospital. Patients, visitors, and employees alike gather around two benches placed on the sides of the two patient entrances to smoke, which creates a cloud of smoke that enters the hospital as patients and visitors come in and out of the entrance doors. For several months, patients, visitors, and even employees have complained about this problem. Several patients with lung problems have pleaded to hospital employees, asking them to do something about the problem.

A few months ago, after hearing the complaints, administrators tried to address the problem. They formed a committee and assigned a project manager to come up with a solution and ways to implement it. The committee consisted of two mid-line managers, two doctors, two employees from the Patient Relations department, and two employees from the Plant Operations department. The committee decided to send out a memo to all units of the hospital, asking the managers to tell their employees not to smoke at patient entrances. They also had a gazebo built outside of the employee entrance and designated its use for employee smoking, which curbed the problem contributed by employees; however, patients and visitors continued smoking at the entrances. After a few months, the committee members were pulled to attend to other problems, interest in the smoking problem declined, and the initiative fizzled out.

The hospital is still having a problem with people smoking at patient entrances. The majority of the contributors to the problem are patients, visitors, and a few doctors, who think that they should not be forced to smoke only at the employee-entrance gazebo. SRMC must address the problem quickly because the hospital will be receiving a visit from JCAHO in two weeks. The administrators have been made aware that JCAHO is cracking down on the presence of smoke at hospital entrances. If smoke is present within the patient entrances when they arrive, the hospital could be fined a significant amount. Administrators are anxious to find a quick and permanent solution to this problem. They want to create a welcoming environment and avoid being fined. They have recently discussed building an additional gazebo designated for patient and visitor smoking; however, they do not have much time and have asked the administrative intern, Julie Gibson, to present a solution.

Julie talked with Harry Floyd, the project manager on the original committee, to get his suggestions on what should be done. Mr. Floyd told her, "I have been working on some sketches for adding a room to the outside of the hospital, which would be designated for smoking." Julie thought, "This idea seems very expensive and unnecessary. And we don't have time to complete such a task. There has to be a less expensive and easier way."

QUESTIONS FOR DISCUSSION

1. In this case, how does the environment of the organization affect patient satisfaction?
2. What kind of emphasis did the administrators of the hospital put on the smoking problem?
3. In your opinion, should Julie recommend solving the problem by building a gazebo or an additional room or is there a better way?
4. What role did the JCAHO play in again mobilizing an effort?

PART SIX

Group Behavior
and Teams

Case 12: Piecing It Together

- ☐ *Group Behavior and Teams*
- ◇ *Communication*
- ◯ *Health Services Research Center*

FOCUSED TOPIC DESCRIPTION

This case focuses on the importance of communication, cooperation, and leadership in creating an effective and cohesive work group in a health services research center.

LEARNING/TEACHING OBJECTIVES

- To develop an understanding of how lack of communication, cooperation, and leadership can create inefficiency and lead to unnecessary stress in a work group and a useless product that reflects the group's lack of cohesiveness
- To highlight the need for periodic review of individual and group responsibilities when performing group tasks

The Healthcare Economics Research Unit (HERU) of Washington Medical Center is located in Washington, D.C. HERU is a small health services research organization with approximately 15 employees. It has a relatively flat organizational structure that includes research assistants, research associates, fellows, and some faculty members from Washington University. All staff report directly to the director. The goal of HERU is to improve healthcare by conducting research that can be used to guide the development and implementation of new healthcare policy.

HERU has just received a contract from Seasile Pharmaceuticals to conduct a study on a new respiratory drug, breatheasymophlabin (BEMP). While this contract in clinical pharmacoeconomics is a departure from HERU's primary focus on health services delivery, it does present an opportunity to develop expertise in an important and rapidly growing domain.

ORGANIZATIONAL PROBLEM

At the weekly research meeting, the director of HERU, Kate Anderson, divided the BEMP project up among the members of the unit according to their specialization. LeMing Cheng, a research associate with a doctorate in economics who has worked at the unit for six years, was asked to evaluate the cost effectiveness of BEMP in comparison to other widely used respiratory drugs. Caren Shaffer, a pharmaceutical fellow who has been with the unit for six months, was asked to evaluate and verify the chemical make up of BEMP. She was also responsible for analyzing the feasibility of BEMP based on drug interactions that may occur between BEMP and other common respiratory drugs. Christina Pallano, a research associate with an MPH, has worked at the unit for four months and was assigned the task of assessing the need for BEMP in different areas around the world. She was asked to develop a marketing plan for BEMP so that Seasile could determine where and how to market its new drug. The researchers had four weeks to complete their tasks and make a presentation to Seasile.

Ms. Shaffer, Mrs. Pallano, and Dr. Cheng decided to meet briefly after the meeting. They quickly came to the consensus that there was not much they could talk about until they had done some more background work on their assignments. They decided to meet again in a week.

At their next meeting, Dr. Cheng showed up late. It was obvious that he was in a hurry and ready to get to the point; he said, "Look guys, I've got a ton of stuff I'm working on right now so let's make this short. None of our topics really go together as far as I see it, so I think we're okay just tackling our own subjects. I've been doing this for awhile and I'm sure that will be fine."

Mrs. Pallano responded, "If you think that's best, I guess it's okay. But, this project was assigned to us as a group and I think we should meet again to make sure we are all on the same page."

"I agree," Ms. Shaffer interjected. "How about if we meet again in two weeks? That will give us plenty of time to prepare the presentation."

At the next weekly unit meeting, Ms. Anderson checked up on all of the researchers. She approved a graph that Dr. Cheng was working on and answered some scientific questions Ms. Shaffer had about BEMP. She also referred Mrs. Pallano to some resources that would help with her marketing research. Ms. Anderson thought that the project was going well and that each of the researchers was doing a thorough job on his or her part.

At the next meeting for the BEMP project, Dr. Cheng took control again. He suggested that they simply agree on what design to use in the PowerPoint presentation software and also determine the order of the presentation. Mrs. Pallano began to get worried. She asked Dr. Cheng, "It sounds as if you're almost done with your part. What exactly are you going to present to Seasile?"

Dr. Cheng responded, "Oh, just some economics stuff. The jargon can be difficult to explain. I'll have lots of charts as usual."

Mrs. Pallano answered, "But, what are you going to say about BEMP?"

Dr. Cheng looked agitated; he retorted, "That it's economically sound and financially feasible, of course. Don't worry; our project will look fine."

Ms. Shaffer looked as if she wanted to say something, but she did not. Later that week, Mrs. Pallano ran into Ms. Shaffer. "I'm a little worried about our presentation. I hope it all matches up," Mrs. Pallano admitted.

"Me too," agreed Ms. Shaffer. "I thought we should talk about our different points of view more. Maybe we should say something to LeMing? But, then again, LeMing has been here for awhile and probably knows what he's doing. If there was something wrong, Kate would have said something by now."

"I guess you're right," Mrs. Pallano answered. "Let's just go with the flow."

Each part of the presentation was completed on time, and the researchers made the presentation to Seasile. Based on Mrs. Pallano's population assessment, BEMP should be marketed in the southern United States. Ms. Shaffer, on the other hand, found that BEMP would have the least amount of drug interactions with respiratory drugs used commonly by South Americans. Unfortunately, Dr. Cheng's economic comparison was based on drug use in the northern United States.

There was good information, but without the appropriate synthesis, the information presented was useless to Seasile. The representatives from Seasile were not pleased with the results. While they found each researcher presented accurate and useful data, they thought that the report was not cohesive enough to benefit their company.

QUESTIONS FOR DISCUSSION

1. Discuss how inefficient communication contributed to the unsatisfactory outcome.
2. What could Ms. Shaffer and Mrs. Pallano have done to prevent this scenario?
3. What could Dr. Cheng have done to prevent this scenario?
4. What role did Ms. Anderson play in creating the problem?
5. What suggestions do you have for assigning or determining leadership roles in a group situation? Explain.

PART SEVEN

Leadership

Case 13: Decisions, Decisions

☐ *Leadership*
◇ *Environment*
◯ *Hospital*

FOCUSED TOPIC DESCRIPTION

This case explores how an organization's internal and external environments influence leadership.

LEARNING/TEACHING OBJECTIVES

- To understand how internal and external environmental changes affect leadership
- To discuss the responsibility and importance of adopting a leadership style that is responsive to employee needs and the demands of the external environment

BACKGROUND AND CASE OVERVIEW

University Memorial Hospitals (UMH) is located in a small, Midwestern college town, which is home to a large state university and teaching hospital. UMH is a 571-bed, state-owned, teaching medical center that employs over 4,000 people. As the primary public hospital in its state, UMH provides tertiary care and specialty services to patients from numerous urban and rural communities. The mission of UMH is to provide high quality patient care, to educate healthcare professionals, to advance health research, and to provide community service. The Planning department's multiple responsibilities include strategic planning, facility planning, and program development.

ORGANIZATIONAL PROBLEM

"Where am I supposed to leave my kids while I'm helping Dr. Smith with patients?" Mary Rogers, a recently hired nursing assistant, asked Tom Martin, manager of the Planning department at UMH. "Here in University Town," she continued, "the daycare facilities are too expensive and inconvenient. Sometimes I have to take time off from work to care for my children. Can't you in Planning do something to remedy that?"

About a year ago, an employee mentioned the idea of a daycare center for hospital employees. Since then, Mr. Martin had been approached repeatedly by aggravated employees, such as Mrs. Rogers, who were dissatisfied with the inadequate supply and high cost of daycare facilities in University Town. As the number of families with both parents who work full-time increased, UMH employees faced greater difficulty in finding suitable care for their children during work hours. Mr. Martin realized that UMH must respond to the changing environment and act as a leader in meeting the needs of its employees. UMH, however, needed to consider a variety of issues before committing to the massive project of building a daycare center.

The CEO of UMH assigned Mr. Martin and Planning the task of determining the advantages and disadvantages of creating a daycare center. Given the large number of UMH employees, the daycare center would have to be able to accommodate a large number of children. If the project seemed feasible, Mr. Martin would also be responsible for developing an acceptable business plan to be presented to UMH's board of directors. He contemplated various ways of approaching this project and decided to create a subcommittee to discuss the pertinent issues and formulate a report for the board. Both UMH and University employees would be invited to participate on the subcommittee to account for the various employee perspectives.

Mr. Martin and his subcommittee considered the possibility of a joint venture between the hospital and the University to build a daycare center in a mutually convenient location. If this option were pursued, UMH and the University would need to collaborate and discuss numerous issues including who would manage the facility, where it would be located, how many slots would be allocated to University versus UMH employees, and what criteria would be used to grant participation to employees.

Mr. Martin wanted to make the best proposal possible for the board, and he was not sure whether he should even recommend building the center. He wondered if UMH overlooked any options that could more effectively meet the daycare needs of employees. He knew the organization needed to respond to the changing environment. In recent months, UMH had consistently experienced increased absenteeism and decreased employee morale. Mr. Martin wondered if the appropriate action was to build a daycare center or if a different approach held the solution.

QUESTIONS FOR DISCUSSION

1. What key issues should Mr. Martin and his subcommittee discuss before developing a proposal for the board?
2. Do you think building a daycare center is an appropriate strategy in response to external environment change? Does this solution address parents' dissatisfaction with

other daycare centers, such as high tuition rates and inconvenience? What further information might you need to make this decision?

3. If the board denied Planning's daycare center proposal, what other options should the department consider to meet the daycare needs of University's employees?

Case 14: Urgent Relief

□ *Leadership*
◇ *Motivation*
○ *Urgent Care Clinic*

FOCUSED TOPIC DESCRIPTION

This case illustrates the importance of having strong day-to-day staff leadership in a dynamic and large hospital facility.

LEARNING/TEACHING OBJECTIVES

- To learn how leadership can affect staff motivation, job performance, and morale
- To evaluate the decision-making role of leadership positions

BACKGROUND AND CASE OVERVIEW

Jamestown University Hospitals (JUH) is a major public academic medical center dedicated to providing high quality patient care, educating healthcare professionals, advancing health research, and providing community service. Located on the campus of Jamestown University in the northeast, this public teaching hospital houses 720 beds. JUH's Urgent Care Center (UCC), an extended hours clinic, is part of the department of Nursing. Its mission is to provide high quality patient care for the treatment of minor, non-acute medical problems in a cohesive, customer-friendly, and affordable manner. Five registered nurses, two nursing assistants, two licensed practical nurses, and two secretaries staff the UCC. Because the UCC is a small operation and has not yet been proven a successful venture through utilization or revenue studies, the department of Nursing has not hired a nurse manager for the UCC staff.

ORGANIZATIONAL PROBLEM

Liza Ross, the chairperson of the department of Nursing, was responsible for all decisions regarding line management of the UCC. After assessing UCC nursing staff needs, Ms. Ross concluded that it was not necessary to hire a full-time nurse manager to supervise such a small staff. Instead, Ms. Ross assigned Julia Moore, the clinical nurse coordinator of the largest of six nursing services in the department, to manage the UCC staff. Ms. Moore willingly accepted the additional responsibility.

Ms. Moore is a diligent, outgoing, and hardworking supervisor with a great deal of responsibility beyond her UCC duties. Since she accepted the responsibility to manage the UCC, she has been a dedicated leader for the nurses and staff and has helped to develop the UCC into a well-known, successful operation. She tries to be available to answer questions and hear suggestions from the UCC staff; however, she admits that she does not have the time available to be at the UCC more than two days a week. She agrees the situation is unfair to UCC staff, but recognizes clearly that her primary role is as clinical nurse coordinator of the Burn and Rehabilitation nursing unit.

About a week after accepting managerial responsibility for the UCC, Ms. Moore suggested to Ms. Ross that Margaret Pabers, the nurse manager of the Emergency department and the Pediatric Acute Care unit, would be an excellent person to manage the UCC until it was operating smoothly. "After all," Ms. Moore reasoned, "the UCC is located directly between the Emergency department and Pediatric Acute Care unit, so it would make sense that Margaret could effectively supervise the UCC staff without much adjustment. Also, Margaret has an outgoing personality and is a very driven person." Ms. Ross agreed that Ms. Moore should speak to Mrs. Pabers about the additional responsibility.

Ms. Moore approached Mrs. Pabers about her idea. Mrs. Pabers welcomed the opportunity to lead the UCC staff, but on a full-time basis: "I think that I am capable of managing an additional staff, and the UCC is right there beside me. There shouldn't be any problem."

However, Ms. Ross was not in favor of appointing Mrs. Pabers to supervise the UCC staff on other than an interim basis. Ms. Ross pointed out that assigning Mrs. Pabers supervision of the UCC staff would give her responsibility over three nursing units, which is more than any other nurse manager in the department. Ms. Ross did not feel that it was wise to give one nurse manager so much responsibility. Although she agreed that Mrs. Pabers might help out on a day-to-day basis, Ms. Ross did not think that it was necessary to create a new position for nurse manager of the UCC. So, the UCC continued to be directed by borrowed and temporary leaders.

The UCC has been growing, with the staff seeing an average of 45 to 55 patient visits per day, which is a 33 percent increase in volume. The nursing staff has done an outstanding job of adhering to the department's strict clinical practice standards and guidelines as well as maintaining a high degree of job satisfaction. The nurses usually look to Janice Dole, the most experienced nurse on the staff, for guidance on day-to-day practice. "I have been working at the UCC since it began, and I worked for 25 years at JUH's walk-in clinic before that," Mrs. Dole explained. "Although I have no formal leadership title, I think the other nurses see me as someone they can look to when neither Julia nor Margaret are around."

Despite Mrs. Dole's informal leadership and support, some of the nurses continue to be frustrated and have begun to complain about the lack of formal leadership at the UCC. They hesitated to approach Ms. Moore with questions or concerns since she is such a busy person. One UCC registered nurse commented, "We understand that Julia is a very busy person. She has a tremendous amount of responsibility and many other people report to her. But, we miss the leadership that a unit supervisor can give us. I know that UCC is too small to have a full-time supervisor, but it would be nice to have a leader we could see everyday."

QUESTIONS FOR DISCUSSION

1. How is leadership in a situation, such as the one described above, related to employee morale and motivation? To job performance and efficiency?
2. What would be the advantages and disadvantages of hiring a nurse manager to lead the UCC staff?
3. What is the best solution for providing the UCC with the leadership it needs without hiring a manager?

PART EIGHT

Motivation, Performance, and Satisfaction

Case 15: Hurry-Home Home Care

☐ *Motivation*
◇ *Organizational Effectiveness*
◎ *Home Health Agency*

FOCUSED TOPIC DESCRIPTION

This case argues that healthcare administrators can use motivational techniques to encourage physicians to utilize home health services.

LEARNING/TEACHING OBJECTIVES

- To determine the role of administration in motivating physicians and staff
- To discuss physicians' influence on organizational effectiveness of home health agencies
- To identify the benefits of utilizing home health services

BACKGROUND AND CASE OVERVIEW

Early discharge from an acute hospital setting is possible if the physician requests continued care through home health services. Home health agencies provide needed services to homebound patients, often at considerable savings for third-party payers.

Hurry-Home Home Care, an affiliate of Long Hospital, is a certified and licensed home health agency located just east of the metropolitan city of Atlanta, Georgia. The agency employs a staff of nurses, medical social workers, home health aides, physical therapists, speech pathologists, occupational therapists, and administrative support staff. Hurry-Home is the primary home health agency that provides services to people in the five surrounding counties.

Before a patient can be seen by Hurry-Home personnel, or become eligible for any home care services, the agency must receive a written referral from the attending physician. Thus, the continued operation of Hurry-Home is dependent on the cooperation and participation of physicians. This is important given the mission of Long Hospital—to provide timely, high-quality patient care. Physicians are, therefore, critical constituencies; they play an integral role in the functioning and overall success of the home health agency. When physicians make a referral for home health services, they do so knowing that they will spend time overseeing the care of the patient without additional compensation. Like other home health agencies and administrators in the industry, Hurry-Home's CEO, Kenneth Bind, has struggled with how to motivate physicians to continue to make these referrals.

ORGANIZATIONAL PROBLEM

Long Hospital's board of directors held a meeting several years ago in which several physicians and community leaders voiced to administrators their complaints about the demands of the home health industry. In the meeting, a group of physicians, led by Dr. Larry Call, threatened to stop making referrals to Hurry-Home.

"Our commitment to patients does not end with the referral," Dr. Call reasoned. "We must be available for consultation

24 hours a day should there be changes in a patient's condition, as well as review and update charts on a regular basis. And that does not even include the time and energy we spend on completing paperwork for third-party payers. We have many extra responsibilities with no compensation."

Paperwork requirements for referring patients to Hurry-Home demand that

- Physicians' orders for all services must be approved and signed;
- Plan of treatment must be written and signed upon admission, and then updated every 60 days; and
- Letters of medical necessity must be written and signed for each case.

"Hurry-Home has taken measures to reduce the demands and obligations placed on physicians," Mr. Bind explained. "Our staff only contact the physician in extreme emergencies. Our staff even attempted to complete some of the required documentation for the physicians. Because of legal restraints and some physicians' refusal to agree to such procedures, the situation has not improved as a result of this effort."

Two days after the meeting, Mr. Bind met with the Hurry-Home staff and asked for suggestions: "We've heard the physicians' reasons for not utilizing our services; what else can we do to encourage their participation?"

QUESTIONS FOR DISCUSSION

1. Discuss the Hurry-Home administration's role in motivating both the hospital physicians and the staff.
2. It is clear that the hospital physicians are a critical constituency of Hurry-Home. What management strategies

would you suggest that Hurry-Home implement so that the physicians will be eager and willing to make referrals for home health services?

3. If internal motivational techniques cannot be used to solve this problem, by what other means can Hurry-Home sustain and improve its efficiency and quality of services?

Case 16: Merit Bonuses at Piney Neurology

☐ *Motivation*
◇ *Decision Making*
◯ *Specialty Clinic*

FOCUSED TOPIC DESCRIPTION

This case explores how decision making can affect employee motivation, employee productivity, and organizational success.

LEARNING/TEACHING OBJECTIVES

- To understand the link between organizational control and employee motivation
- To assess the importance of employee input on changes that affect the work environment
- To consider methods for decreasing employee resistance

BACKGROUND AND CASE OVERVIEW

Piney Neurology is a group practice with a staff of five doctors, one administrator, and 10 support members. Piney Neurology, well known for its excellent medical care and professional staff, offers care to residents in five counties of a Southeastern state. The rapport between the staff and doctors aids in the process of providing the best neurological care to its Southeastern communities.

Changes started to take place at Piney Neurology several months ago. After 15 years of service, the group practice administrator, Ben Glynn, decided to retire. Over the years, Mr. Glynn had always tried to make employees feel welcome and appreciated. The key to his management philosophy was to promote good relationships between the staff and doctors. One of his favorite tasks was passing out annual employee bonuses, which were given to staff based on seniority. Mr. Glynn thought that this reward system was an appropriate way of recognizing the staff for the work they had done throughout the year. Upon the announcement of his retirement, the physicians at Piney Neurology initiated an extensive search for a new office administrator.

ORGANIZATIONAL PROBLEM

At the weekly office meeting, Dr. Steve Leaman, one of the physicians at Piney Neurology, led the discussion about the vacant position. He and the other four doctors discussed the skills and characteristics they wanted in a new administrator.

"There should be more authority over the staff here at our clinic. In the past year, the quality of our support staff has significantly declined. Several staff members have become inefficient and unreliable in completing their daily tasks," Dr. Michelle Coleman complained. "Why, just the other day, Janet Estes came in 10 minutes late from her lunch break and then proceeded to take a five-minute restroom break! It was not the first time that has happened."

"I agree with you," said Dr. Bill Meade. "Some employees were standing around socializing in the coffee room last Wednesday, and it wasn't even break time. When I walked by they all got to work in a hurry."

"There has to be a way to improve the staff's attitude when it comes to work," said Dr. Janet Green. "I think we need to hit them where it hurts most—in the pocket! When Ben was administrator, he passed out bonuses like they were candy, without considering the quality of employees' work. If we continue to hand out bonuses like that without considering work performance, our practice and its reputation may be in jeopardy."

Dr. Leaman and the other doctors agreed that they needed to develop a new method for distributing bonuses for the current fiscal year. They decided to make employee bonuses a top issue during the interviews with potential office administrators. After two months of rigorous interviews, William Bushnell was hired as the new administrator. His extensive experience in human resources management and view on staff bonuses were determining factors in his selection.

During his first month, Mr. Bushnell developed an innovative approach for distributing staff bonuses. After much deliberation with the physicians, he implemented a four-step plan that would create a standard performance appraisal for staff. First, he and the physicians would evaluate each employee individually. Second, the evaluation scores would be averaged. Third, employees would be ranked according to their final score. Fourth, employees would be evaluated on completion of tasks, efficiency, attitude, and general work appearance. Mr. Bushnell and the physicians were excited about the new plan and were confident about the positive effects it would have on employee work performance. He called a staff meeting to explain the new evaluation process to everyone. He outlined the four-step plan and encouraged staff not to worry. His presentation, however, was not greeted with excitement. In fact, none of the employees seemed receptive to the new evaluation method and most appeared angry and resentful.

"So, I haven't been doing my job well enough, and bonuses were wasted on me in the past?" barked a 10-year veteran staff member.

"I can't believe this. I spend an hour getting ready to come here every morning. They better not tell me that my appearance is not pleasing," said another staff member.

Another employee mournfully said, "Mr. Glynn would have never done this without getting our input first. I need that bonus check to get through the rest of the year!"

Mr. Bushnell was oblivious to the uproar that he and the physicians had caused, and, with the physicians' support, proceeded with the end-of-year evaluations. He met individually with staff members to discuss their results and scores, stressed each employee's strengths and weaknesses, and emphasized their importance at Piney Neurology. He also offered suggestions for improving their performance. At the close of each evaluation, Mr. Bushnell distributed the bonus checks with a parting remark, "I want us all to be a team. But to do that, we all need to be team players. In other words, don't go out in the office and share how much your bonus is. We want this to be a reflection on you as an individual, not on the team as a whole."

The next day, Janet Estes gave her two-week notice of resignation. She had been the head secretary at Piney Neurology for 10 years and was well respected by other staff members. Her reason for leaving was simple. After talking with other employees, she discovered that her bonus was lower than any other staff member. She felt that her bonus reflected neither her loyalty to the organization nor the amount of work that she had accomplished over the past year.

QUESTIONS FOR DISCUSSION

1. Why did the physicians think that the evaluation procedure for bonuses needed to be changed?
2. Why was there resistance to changing the evaluation procedure for bonuses?
3. To better motivate the employees, how could a new employee evaluation procedure be implemented?

PART NINE

Organizational Change

Case 17: A Focus on Departmental Downsizing

☐ *Organizational Change*
◇ *Decision Making*
◯ *Hospital*

FOCUSED TOPIC DESCRIPTION

This case focuses on identifying organizational changes that can improve organizational efficiency.

LEARNING/TEACHING OBJECTIVES

- To understand how organizational change, such as organizational restructuring, can improve efficiency
- To understand the benefits of utilizing a collective decision-making process in restructuring an organization

BACKGROUND AND CASE OVERVIEW

Get Well Hospital, located in an East Coast community, is a large, not-for-profit, teaching hospital that offers a wide array of services to its patients. Within the hospital, the Cost Accounting (CA) department has sole responsibility for determining service price, evaluating procedures for cost effectiveness, and creating the annual Medicare cost report. CA follows Get Well Hospital's mission—to ensure patient satisfaction and advance healthcare research and technology by providing high quality, cost effective services at an affordable price. CA has four divisions—Budget, Reimbursement, Audit, and Costing. Each division has its own staff—one manager and multiple assistant managers—who reports directly to the director and assistant director of CA. The director of the CA, Jeff Koon, reports directly to the CFO of Get Well Hospital and is responsible for maintaining the efficient coordination and interaction among these four divisions.

ORGANIZATIONAL PROBLEM

At the beginning of the fiscal year, Mr. Koon, who had just returned from a total quality management (TQM) seminar, analyzed CA's managerial staff composition. He noticed that there was a reduction in output among the middle management staff in the Audit and Reimbursement divisions. A number of these managers had been with the hospital for over 20 years. Mr. Koon wondered if many of these upper-level management positions were necessary given the recent internal structure improvements in technology and CA's need for improved efficiency to remain competitive in the external environment. To further analyze the issue, he developed and distributed surveys to all employees in the four divisions to inquire about their relationships and interactions with middle management.

The responses he received indicated that employees felt distanced from their supervisors. There appeared to be a poor communication flow among divisions, and employees felt they did the majority of the work while management received all the credit. Another response to the survey was that employees of the

Audit and Reimbursement divisions had difficulty keeping a consistent and timely flow of resources and materials among divisions. This was an especially critical function during the Medicare cost reporting season, when the Costing division depends heavily on combined information from both the Audit and Reimbursement divisions.

After considering the results of the survey, Mr. Koon held a management meeting to discuss CA's structural problems. "I received some distressing feedback from employees that indicates our systems approach and high degree of vertical structure may no longer be optimal," he informed the division managers. "I have outlined a few of the main problems that I have been able to identify. I would like for us all to brainstorm for solutions."

He outlined the problems as follows.

- Inefficient coordination and completion of the product transformation process involving the Audit, Reimbursement, and Costing divisions
- Diminished communication between division managers and employees
- Uneven division of labor between managers and employees, as well as among divisions

"Do you see these same problems at the management level?" Mr. Koon asked the division managers.

The Audit division manager responded, "Yes, I see all of these issues as problems. I especially think that our division does an enormous amount of preliminary calculations that the Reimbursement division could assist us in completing."

The Costing division manager agreed, "I think the main reason for the difficulty in communication and uneven workload is the result of too much divisional specialization. Also, by having division managers and divisional assistant managers, we increase the channels that communication and work must flow through. This degree of vertical depth is not necessary and inhibits the timeliness in completing divisional outputs."

After a lengthy discussion, Mr. Koon concluded the meeting by asking the management to meet with employees in their respective divisions and gather ideas for solving these problems. He said, "I would like to meet again next week with the goal of creating a solution that satisfies both employees and management, as well as one that promotes division efficiency."

QUESTIONS FOR DISCUSSION

1. Do you think Mr. Koon employed a fair and effective organizational change strategy to address CA's structural problems? What were the strengths and weaknesses of this strategy?
2. What strategies should be employed to increase the communication and coordination of communication among and within divisions?
3. What strategies could be effective in creating a more evenly distributed workload among and within divisions?
4. Would it be realistic to combine the strategies in Questions 2 and 3 in a way that minimizes the negative effects of organizational restructure? What would be an effective way to combine these strategies?

Case 18: Beach Memorial Hospital

☐ *Organizational Change*
◇ *Conflict and Negotiation*
◯ *Hospital*

FOCUSED TOPIC DESCRIPTION

This case purports that organizational change, including organizational restructuring, is often required to meet the objectives of an organization.

LEARNING/TEACHING OBJECTIVES

- To distinguish how organizational determinants can create a need for organizational change
- To understand how employee management relations affect all aspects of an organization
- To identify the various options available in establishing leadership roles in a new facility

BACKGROUND AND CASE OVERVIEW

Beach Memorial Hospital (BMH), located in the Pacific Northwest, provides services for a rapidly growing city and its surrounding rural communities. Morgantown is a medium-sized urban coastal city with a population of approximately 50,000. Psychiatric services, offered by BMH, are one of the most utilized services in the area; the only other psychiatric hospital in Morgantown is located about 20 minutes away in a neighboring town. Therefore, BMH must continually evaluate the performance of its Psychiatric department and strive to improve quality to achieve its mission of providing the highest quality care to its patients.

ORGANIZATIONAL PROBLEM

After distributing an employee satisfaction survey, the CEO of BMH, Sandy Shores, MBA, discovered three major problems within the psychiatric department:

1. Inadequate space and an institutional atmosphere
2. Outdated technologies
3. Poor employee–manager relations

These problems were creating tension and frustration among employees, which, as a result, hinder their ability to fulfill BMH's mission. Ms. Shores had also heard from employees that patients were uncomfortable coming in for appointments because the Psychiatric department was located in a high traffic area adjacent to the Obstetrics and Gynecology (OB/GYN) department. While psychiatric patients sat in the waiting room for their appointments, expecting mothers, new parents, and others walked by to the OB/GYN department.

Based on the information obtained from the surveys and employee feedback, Ms. Shores decided to restructure the Psychiatric department. She was convinced that it should be converted into its own facility located in a separate building on BMH's medical campus and equipped with its own entrance and parking area. Ms. Shores held a meeting with BMH's department chairs to introduce the idea and solicit feedback. She provided statistics that demonstrate the poor performance of the department and enumerated several reasons that it would benefit from operating as a separate facility, including:

- Decreasing the likelihood of stigmatization by keeping the psychiatric patients separate from other hospital patients;
- Creating a more home-like environment for patients; and
- Accommodating the projected increase in demand for psychiatric services.

"Patients are more likely to seek psychiatric services if they aren't scared of running into their neighbor while passing through other departments on the way to the Psychiatric department," Ms. Shores explained. "Patients need a warm atmosphere to comfort their emotional and mental suffering. Furthermore, the Psychiatric department does not have enough space to accommodate the current patient load, much less the capacity to support the projected increase."

The staff was receptive to Ms. Shores's reasoning and supported moving forward with the change. The only opposition came from the department chair of Psychiatric Services, Ima Meggs. She knew that she was not well liked or respected by departmental employees and felt threatened by the structural change. Also, she had some concerns about the effect of the restructuring on professional relationships.

"I don't see what the employees' fuss is all about. I wish they would be less concerned with the space in which they work and just do the work that I have assigned," Ms. Meggs complained. "I have been with BMH for 23 years and, frankly, I like the way the organization is structured. This restructuring would also have a serious negative effect on our professional relationships with other departments and the integration of mental health services with other clinical disciplines. If we are located in a separate building, we will not have as much contact with our colleagues in other departments. Don't you see that we should all work together to care for patients? If the Cardiology department has a patient recovering from heart surgery who is very depressed and was referred to our department, how are we to collaborate with the cardiologist to provide a seamless continuum of care?"

When BMH decided to move forward with Ms. Shores's recommendations, Ms. Meggs turned in her resignation. Based on the mainly positive feedback from the staff, Ms. Shores asked, "Now that we have the feedback and support of BMH employees, how can we make these ideas a reality?"

QUESTIONS FOR DISCUSSION

1. What are the determinants leading to the need for change at Beach Memorial Hospital? Why should management be concerned with the effects of these determinants?
2. Organizations are often very resistant to change. What strategies could be used to deal with this resistance?
3. Because of Ms. Meggs's resignation, Ms. Shores must consider whether or not to change the management structure. What options should she consider?

PART TEN

Organizational Culture

Case 19: Global Culture in the Workplace

▢ *Organizational Culture*
◇ *Communication*
◎ *Hospital*

FOCUSED TOPIC DESCRIPTION

This case supports recognizing and accommodating global cultural work ethics in organizations.

LEARNING/TEACHING OBJECTIVES

- To recognize some of the strengths of the work ethic of employees from other cultures in an American health-care setting
- To demonstrate how different language and cultural patterns can negatively affect patient–provider communication despite good intentions
- To identify ways to accommodate differences between foreign and domestic work ethics

BACKGROUND AND CASE OVERVIEW

UCT Hospitals is a 672-bed academic medical center and teaching hospital. Located in Center Town, Georgia, the hospital serves patients from all of the state's counties. The mission of UCT is to provide high-quality patient care, to educate health-care professionals, to advance health research, and to provide community service. UCT's Neurosurgery Clinic has done very well in upholding the hospital's mission through its devotion to patient education.

In recent years, there has been a substantial number of foreign medical school residents who arrive to practice at UCT. Because of the high quality of education and the diverse cultural environment, many formal foreign physicians have been attracted to UCT. The Neurosurgery Clinic participates in a foreign exchange program with Japan. This program permits Japanese medical school residents to practice in an American hospital setting. So far, UCT has also found it advantageous to house Japanese physicians because of their devotion and commitment to the norms and values of the hospital. More than one person has commented on how Japanese doctors tend to be more supportive of group efforts to promote quality of patient care. In that perspective, they are distinctly unlike the individualistic American doctors. One Japanese doctor in particular, Dr. Paul Chan, has even tried to initiate a quality circle for the Neurosurgery Clinic.

ORGANIZATIONAL PROBLEM

Over the past few months, the clinic manager of the Neurosurgery Clinic, Freda Jackson, has received a number of complaints about the clinic. Because the clinic prides itself on excellence, the complaints were a surprise. Even more surprising is that the focus of the complaints seemed to center on the services provided by Dr. Chan. Patients complained that they were not getting enough information and education about their neurological procedure and they found him aloof. Dr. Chan could speak English, but it is broken and sometimes hard to understand. When Mrs. Jackson talked to one of Dr. Chan's patients, the patient admitted, "I can't understand what Dr. Chan is talking about, and I'm scared that I will miss something that I should know about my condition."

Recognizing the communication barrier between Dr. Chan and his patients, Mrs. Jackson decided to discuss the problem with other clinic managers in the hospital. During a clinic managers' meeting, Mrs. Jackson stressed the importance of Dr. Chan's team leadership and devotion to the organization. However, she also mentioned that UCT must uphold its mission to provide high quality care to its patients. What can Freda do to resolve this problem?

QUESTIONS FOR DISCUSSION

1. How could behaviors of foreign organizational culture bring efficiency to an American organization?
2. How does Dr. Chan's cultural difference affect patient care? Positively? Negatively?
3. What options does Mrs. Jackson have in this situation? Which option would you choose if you were the clinic manager?
4. Have you encountered a situation similar to this one? How were the difficulties resolved?

Case 20: No Time to Waste

☐ *Organizational Culture*
◇ *Organizational Effectiveness*
◯ *Consulting Firm*

FOCUSED TOPIC DESCRIPTION

This case discusses the importance of the internal culture of consulting firms and how it may impinge on individual lifestyles.

LEARNING/TEACHING OBJECTIVES

- To understand the relationship between organizational behavior and organizational effectiveness
- To examine the organizational culture within a consulting firm
- To examine personal lifestyle issues and career paths for consultants

BACKGROUND AND CASE OVERVIEW

Blalock & Chipman Consulting is a small healthcare consulting firm located in Washington, D.C. The firm was founded 11 years ago and has been providing consulting assistance to health service organizations since. The firm has 13 employees, 11 of whom work directly on projects; the other two employees are secretaries—Linda Lee and John Kodiac.

One of Blalock & Chipman's largest clients is the Department of Health and Human Services for the state of Virginia. The state contracted with Blalock & Chipman consultants to devise a plan for implementing use of the Medicare managed care plan—Medicare+Choice—by Virginians who currently receive Medicare. Presently, the state allows Medicare recipients to either enroll in the Medicare+Choice plan or stay with their current traditional Medicare plan.

Sally Halvertson and Michelle Cole are the Blalock & Chipman consultants assigned to the project. Ms. Halvertson has worked for the firm for almost 10 years and received her MBA degree prior to coming to Blalock & Chipman. Ms. Cole, on the other hand, has only recently joined the firm and has a bachelor's degree in health administration and eight years of consulting experience.

Both Ms. Halvertson and Ms. Cole have been working on the project for over six months and have been very dedicated to making sure that every deadline for the project has been met. They both know that this is a very important long-term project for the firm so they are ready to meet whatever demand the state imposes.

The state employee who oversees the project is Kevin Miller. Mr. Miller is pleased with progress on the implementation plan that the Blalock & Chipman consultants have made so far. In particular, he has been impressed with the quality of dedication that Ms. Halvertson and Ms. Cole have brought to the assignment. Every time he has made a request, he has never worried about its arrival. Although the firm is four hours away, he knows that Ms. Halvertson and Ms. Cole will complete his request and have it delivered to him the next day.

ORGANIZATIONAL PROBLEM

At 4:00 p.m. on Wednesday, Ms. Halvertson received a call from Mr. Miller—he needed a report for a presentation at 1:00 p.m. on Friday. Ms. Halvertson projected that preparing and completing the report would take four to five hours. Because the report had to be given to Federal Express on Thursday morning to meet Mr. Miller's deadline, the request meant that they had to stay late that night.

Ms. Halvertson and Ms. Cole worked diligently on the report, and by 10:00 p.m. it was ready to be sent. Both were tired but were relieved to have once again completed a project before the scheduled deadline. They knew Mr. Miller would be pleased.

On their way out, Ms. Halvertson put the report in a Federal Express envelope and placed it on Linda's desk with a note requesting that the envelope be mailed in the morning. Ms. Halvertson was a little nervous about leaving it on Linda's desk because Linda had only recently been hired and may not be as familiar with office procedure as John, who would not be in the office on Thursday. After leaving the package, both Ms. Halvertson and Ms. Cole headed home. Both were going to be out of the office on Thursday for a new project in a neighboring town.

On Friday morning, Ms. Halvertson returned to the office and found the Federal express envelope still sitting on Linda's desk. Shocked, she took it to Ms. Cole immediately.

"Michelle, what are we going to do? We have a huge problem on our hands!" Ms. Halvertson cried out as she held up the envelope. She and Ms. Cole exchanged surprised looks and each instinctively realized what the next step had to be.

Ms. Cole took a deep breath and harshly asked, "Where is she? I want to know exactly how she is going to explain this. No, I don't have time for excuses. I have a report to deliver by one. We have to leave immediately if we're going to make it on time.

We'll just have to tackle the rural health project when we get back."

"John, explain to everyone where we are," Ms. Halvertson called out. "Oh, and if you get a chance, tell Linda that we need to meet briefly as soon as Sally and I return."

Ms. Halvertson and Ms. Cole drove the report to the Virginia office and handed it to Mr. Miller by 12:30 p.m. It was a close call. Both consultants spent the entire day traveling and lost a day of work to do a job that Federal Express could have completed much more easily.

QUESTIONS FOR DISCUSSION

1. Did Ms. Halvertson and Ms. Cole err in choosing to make the delivery by car? in accepting the assignment?
2. Why did Linda not understand the urgency of getting the envelope out?
3. How does a consulting firm talk about its organizational behavior/organizational culture? Are the messages about the firm implicit or explicit?
4. Career path question: Why do graduates often choose a career in consulting? for how long? what is the next logical career step?

Case 21: Parlez-Vous Français?

☐ *Organizational Culture*
◇ *Communication*
◎ *Health Services Research Center*

FOCUSED TOPIC DESCRIPTION

This case illustrates difficulties encountered because of language barriers in an organization and gives suggestions on how to deal with different organizational cultures.

LEARNING/TEACHING OBJECTIVES

- To recognize the risks posed to organizational effectiveness by language barriers
- To learn to deal with language barriers in an organization
- To develop tolerance and appreciation for different organizational cultures
- To learn the importance of proper communication in an organization

BACKGROUND AND CASE OVERVIEW

The division of Health Research is a research division of Napoleon Hospital located in Saint-Urban, Quebec, Canada. The division conducts cross-disciplinary research on key health topics and publishes findings in both professional journals and the lay press. The division's goal is to increase public awareness of and promote prevention programs for prevalent Canadian health conditions.

The majority of the employees in the division are bilingual, speaking both French and English; however, not everyone is equally fluent in both languages. This can potentially lead to problems in the organization. While research is often conducted in a bilingual environment, reports are written in English first and then later translated into French. The research is usually conducted by cross-disciplinary teams formed to take advantage of the multiple skills of the division's staff. Staff members are assigned individual tasks to complete, but consistent, open communication among group members is essential to the final quality of the research.

ORGANIZATIONAL PROBLEM

Last December, Joe Miller, a graduate of the University of South Carolina, accepted a position as a research assistant at the division. Although Joe had studied French in high school and had completed intermediate language studies as an undergraduate in college, he was not fluent. On his first day of work, the division chair, Dr. Jacques Allard, suggested to the entire research staff to go to lunch to welcome Joe. At lunch, Joe sat next to Dr. Allard, who spoke to him in accented English, but the others who sat closer to him spoke French during most of the lunch. Joe had not anticipated this; he struggled to communicate. He answered people's questions the best he could, but often responded with *"Je ne parle très bien français"* (I do not speak French very well). As the lunch wore on, Joe noticed that some of the staff seated on the other side of the table were speaking English.

As weeks passed, Joe noticed that staff tended to cluster into two distinct groups: those whose first language was English and those who were more comfortable speaking French. Misunderstandings occurred often because the use of both languages tended to cluster information and people. These misunderstandings tended to translate into gaps in input, analysis, and reporting on the division's research projects. Although about 60 percent of the employees were bilingual, many, like Joe, had a strong preference for one language over the other. Daily meetings were held to discuss projects and were held in both languages in a good attempt to improve understanding among staff. Inevitably, however, someone would neglect to translate some detail for someone else, and often that small detail was an important one. Some of the researchers frequently left the meetings confused and frustrated.

At one of the daily meetings to review progress on an evaluation of the long-term effects on the liver of underage drinking, Dr. Allard assigned Joe to write a literature review and Marie, a French speaker, to conduct cross-continental telephone surveys of epidemiologists across Canada. Because Dr. Allard gave the instructions in French, Joe was confused about his assignment. He and Marie both spent the day calling epidemiologists. At the end of the day when Joe and Marie reported to Dr. Allard, they realized simultaneously that the same task was done twice. Dr. Allard was upset and angry because of the excess cost to the division's phone bill and because the literature review had not been started. He made both Joe and Marie work late without additional compensation to complete the literature review together. Joe, Marie, and Dr. Allard were frustrated with the incident, but were a bit uncertain about how to avoid future misunderstandings.

QUESTIONS FOR DISCUSSION

1. Describe the problem and the various factors that con-
    tribute to it.
2. What could the people involved in the incident—Joe,
    Marie, and Dr. Allard—have done differently to avoid
    the problem?
3. How can the division structure its meetings differently to
    prevent the recurrence of this type of incident?
4. List events or activities that might help integrate the two
    language groups in the division.

Case 22: The Fine Balance Between Having Fun and Getting the Work Done

☐ *Organizational Culture*
◇ *Organizational Structure*
○ *Government*

FOCUSED TOPIC DESCRIPTION

This case illustrates how an organization's culture can have detrimental and positive effects on employee performance.

LEARNING/TEACHING OBJECTIVE

- To understand how organizational culture can affect organizational effectiveness

BACKGROUND AND CASE OVERVIEW

The Senator of Georgia has three offices—one in Washington, D.C., and two in Georgia. The Washington, D.C., office has 26 employees who support the Senator and his legislative agenda—

they advise him on how legislative proposals will affect Georgia and respond to constituent needs and requests.

Within the office, there are two structural divisions of staff members. One division focuses on legislation while the other focuses on constituents. Although the legislative staff members are highly trained experts in specific disciplines, they share a common set of beliefs and a subculture that emphasizes professionalism within a friendly atmosphere. The age, experience, and enormous workload of these staff members augment this level of professionalism.

In contrast to the highly professional subculture of the legislative staff members, the constituent service division is extremely informal. Specific job tasks for constituent service staff members include handling constituent mail and requests and responses from the Senator. Several factors contribute to the informal climate and subculture of the constituent service staff. First, the majority of them are young—most are recent college graduates under 24 years old. Second, many do not have a social circle outside of the division. Third, many of the division's daily tasks do not involve much critical thinking, which leaves the staff ample time for social interaction.

ORGANIZATIONAL PROBLEM

In the beginning of May, eight college students arrived on Capitol Hill to participate in the senator's summer internship program. They were immediately immersed in the subculture of the constituent service division. Strong group rapport developed because each of the eight interns instantly felt comfortable with the staff members who were in the same age group and stage in life. The constituent service staff members even invited the interns to join the Senate softball league team.

Amid this friendly and comfortable subculture, problems started to develop. The first problem was the lack of interesting work available for the interns. The constituent service staff successfully handled requests nine months of the year and viewed the summer as a time to be free of the monotonous tasks; so, when the interns arrived, they were assigned the unglamorous grunt work. This had been a problem in the past, but for some reason it seemed particularly acute this summer. The second problem was that although the age difference was slight, a significant difference in status and authority was apparent between staff and interns.

Nathan, a graduate student intern, began to take unfair advantage of the relaxed subculture. He came to work late, left early, and spent most of his time in the office surfing the Internet. He resented the menial tasks that were assigned to him and did not respect the authority of the intern coordinator, Shannon, who was only two years his senior. Shannon informally mentioned to Nathan her concern about his inappropriate behavior, but Nathan ignored Shannon's concern and made no effort to change his attitude or performance. After several weeks, a major blowout occurred between Nathan and Shannon.

"Nathan, could you please reorganize the constituent file system?" Shannon asked. "I know it's not a fun job, but it needs to be done."

"I'm here for educational purposes and to further my career. I need to spend my time networking with other Senate staff members and doing Internet research," Nathan snapped. "Let the undergrad interns handle the file system!"

"Nathan, I asked you to do this task, and I expect it to be done by tomorrow at the close of business," ordered Shannon. "Also, let me remind you that you are paid for working from nine to six, not from ten-thirty to three."

Nathan refused to respond to Shannon's comment. Shannon became so frustrated that she ordered him not to return on Monday and not to complete the full six weeks of his internship.

QUESTIONS FOR DISCUSSION

1. How did the constituent service division's subculture interfere with employee performance?
2. What alternative supervisory strategies might Shannon have used to resolve the problem without jeopardizing the informal culture of the division?
3. What additional steps could be taken at the organizational level to maintain a friendly and relaxed subculture and avoid the problems found in this case study?
4. Describe the impact that the office's structure had on its subcultures.

PART ELEVEN

Organizational Goals
and Effectiveness

Case 23: Organizational Effectiveness at U.S. Better Housing Department

- ☐ *Organizational Effectiveness*
- ◇ *Conflict*
- ◎ *Government*

FOCUSED TOPIC DESCRIPTION

This case exemplifies how conflict between two individuals in an office can result in organizational ineffectiveness that affect many other employees.

LEARNING/TEACHING OBJECTIVES

- To understand the role of information management and communication in promoting organizational effectiveness
- To understand that managers and director behaviors affect the effectiveness of all employees they supervise

BACKGROUND AND CASE OVERVIEW

The U.S. government has established a variety of agencies that deal with issues ranging from healthcare to energy to education. These agencies are massive, bureaucratic organizations characterized by a high degree of centralization and formalization. In the spring of her junior year at Yukon State College, Sally Riedel had the opportunity to intern at the U.S. Better Housing Department (USBHD). USBHD's mission is to meet the nation's need for 1) decent housing for all Americans and 2) sound community development consonant with national goals and policies. Sally interned at a USBHD office that works toward encouraging institutions of higher education to become involved in the achievement of USBHD's mission.

ORGANIZATIONAL PROBLEM

Because of USBHD's enormous size, specific policies and procedures for daily operation are critical to the organization's effectiveness. In Sally's office, tasks are often subdivided and allocated down the organization's rank and file, while ideas are channeled up to the upper management for review and consideration. Problems arise within the organization when this two-way avenue becomes bogged down with an excess of suggestions and assignments. Sally quickly discovered the negative results of such an occurrence.

The office where Sally works attempts to improve communications between institutions of higher education and their surrounding communities. The director, Robert Johnson, and two grant specialists, Rudy Luallen and Joyce Stires, were responsible for assigning tasks to Sally and the other summer intern. The communication between the grant specialists was minimal at best.

One afternoon, Mr. Luallen gave Sally a stack of grant progress reports to read and asked her to summarize them in a Lotus spreadsheet. Later that day, Ms. Stires told Sally to call every state and regional office to make sure a faxed memo was received and the responses were forthcoming. When Sally told Ms. Stires about her work for Mr. Luallen, Ms. Stires said, "It's okay to put that aside for now and work on this project." Sally followed her instructions and began calling the offices.

Before the end of the day, Mr. Luallen asked Sally how many reports she had entered. After Sally told him about the assignment switch, Mr. Luallen grumbled, "Joyce often oversteps her boundaries!" Ms. Stires was in her office and overheard the comment and because she was Mr. Luallen's senior by 26 years, she thought that she had a higher priority when it came to assigning work to interns.

To complicate matters, the director, Mr. Johnson, was more a figurehead for USBHD rather than an actual manager for Sally. (USBHD awards the position of director on a one-year rotating basis to a college professor.) Sally did not know to whom to turn for advice; she had learned that going to either Ms. Stires or Mr. Luallen would lead her in circles. Sally thought that the quality of her work would soon suffer if she did not work out this conflict.

QUESTIONS FOR DISCUSSION

1. What organizational effectiveness criteria does this U.S. Better Housing Department (USBHD) office fail to meet?
2. Does USBHD adequately meet its assessment criteria?
3. What might the director do differently to help the office avoid this type of conflict in the future?

Case 24: Staying Alive

☐ *Organizational Effectiveness*
◇ *Organizational Life Cycle*
◯ *Home Health Agency*

FOCUSED TOPIC DESCRIPTION

This case argues that improvements in organizational effectiveness often require organizational change.

LEARNING/TEACHING OBJECTIVES

- To recognize the major components of organizational effectiveness within a small health service organization
- To explore the relationship between organizational effectiveness and organizational change
- To identify new methods for problem solving

BACKGROUND AND CASE OVERVIEW

Circle of Care is located in the largest city in the Appalachian mountain range. Four hospitals and an array of organizations together provide a full continuum of care to this mountain community. Circle of Care is a not-for-profit pediatric program that operates as a joint venture between Visiting Health Professionals and Mountain Area Hospice. The mission of Circle of Care encompasses three goals: 1) to facilitate communication between healthcare providers, 2) to offer guidance in the transition from hospital care to home care, and 3) to help families become skilled care providers and advocates for the needs of their children.

With a staff of only 14, Circle of Care has made 450 home health visits since its establishment two years ago. Part of this success is because of the strong relationships that exist between Circle of Care and the Neonatal Intensive Care unit at Memorial Hospital and with area pediatrician practices. The rapport built through these relationships and the exemplary quality of care have contributed to a dramatic increase in referrals. Another reason for Circle of Care's success during the early stages of its growth is the dedication of its staff. Although a higher number of referrals can be advantageous for a thriving business, it imposes a greater demand on staff's energy. Circle of Care projects that its prospective population includes at least 180 medically fragile children in a six-county area. Despite its dedicated staff of LPNs, RNs, therapists, and administrative/support personnel, Circle of Care faces limited human resources for the projected demand for services.

ORGANIZATIONAL PROBLEM

"I enjoy working with the children and their families, but I simply cannot complete my work in 48 hours every weekend, especially not as the single RN on call," Clark Carpenter, the only official weekend RN, explained at the staff meeting.

Sherra Brokaw, the Human Resources manager, called the meeting to discuss the weekend workload with all employees.

Weekend visits were initially minimal when Circle of Care began operation, so Mrs. Brokaw had projected that only one RN was needed for coverage. However, there has been almost a 16 percent increase in weekend referrals lately and Clark was beginning to be overwhelmed.

"Not only do I perform an average of 12.5 visits per weekend, but I have to spend half of my time staying up to date with documentation," Clark continued. Although he did not say so, the thought of resigning had crossed his mind more than once.

After the meeting, Sherra considered the history and changing trend of weekend visits since Circle of Care's beginning. Between October 1 and June 7, 83 percent of weekends had required additional coverage, which necessitated at least one additional employee. In those cases, Mrs. Brokaw usually pulled weekday staff to fill gaps in weekend coverage and paperwork. While most employees assumed that this shift of responsibility would be temporary, it had become an almost routine practice. Weekday employees were becoming burned out because they were repeatedly required to perform seven-day workweeks.

"Increased turnover is causing setbacks because of required training time, orientation, and changes in benefits. Even though we offer $30 of incentive pay per visit to weekday employees who work on weekends, the frustration level among the workers is increasing because everyone feels overwhelmed," Mrs. Brokaw thought. "I can't sit back and watch my entire staff resign."

Mrs. Brokaw understood when she began working with Circle of Care that problems would inevitably arise because the organization was new and was still determining its service and staffing needs. However, she was concerned about maintaining the standard of care without having to turn patients away. By failing to adequately meet the needs of the community, she was afraid there would be a decline in future referrals.

QUESTIONS FOR DISCUSSION

1. What are the key indicators of organizational effectiveness used by Circle of Care?
2. Are there other indicators that could be used to help
   decrease the level of staff frustration?
3. What long-term and short-term changes would you
   suggest? If Mrs. Brokaw does not implement a change to
   improve effectiveness, what impact could this have on
   Circle of Care?

Case 25: Where's the Paper?

☐ *Organizational Effectiveness*
◇ *Customers and the Environmental Domain*
◎ *Assisted Living Facility*

FOCUSED TOPIC DESCRIPTION

This case demonstrates how job dissatisfaction for employees of
assisted living facilities can affect internalization of organizational
goals and other criteria for organizational effectiveness.

LEARNING/TEACHING OBJECTIVES

- To evaluate the role of employees in ensuring organizational effectiveness
- To determine methods for allowing customers/residents to voice complaints
- To learn how distrust between management and employees can negatively affect customer satisfaction
- To understand the importance of customer satisfaction for retaining residents at an assisted living facility

BACKGROUND AND CASE OVERVIEW

Aged in Place Assisted Living (APAL) is a for-profit assisted living home with 120 residents located in a small community in eastern Virginia. The mission of APAL is to provide high-quality service and care to all residents of its community.

APAL was once the only "true" assisted living home for the community. However, because of the "elderly gold rush" and the rapid growth of the industry, APAL now has to compete with four modern assisted living homes located within five miles of its current location. These four facilities have opened periodically over the past six-and-a-half years. Residents and families who are not satisfied with services provided by APAL now have the option of moving to one of these other facilities.

At APAL and other assisted living settings, certified nursing assistants (CNAs) are the front-line offense in providing quality care to satisfy the residents. Unfortunately, most CNAs have minimal levels of education and are not paid well. In addition, they are often afraid to speak to management about problems because they are worried that they might lose their job. Most CNAs tend to ignore problems they confront at APAL and simply continue to go on. Because of these fears, developing trust between management and hourly staff is an on-going challenge for the APAL management team. Because of the opening of new assisted living homes in the community, a second related, and increasingly urgent, challenge to APAL is retaining both residents and reliable staff.

ORGANIZATIONAL PROBLEM

Gloria Maye, an 83-year-old widow who lives at APAL, awoke one morning to find out that her newspaper had not been delivered to her room. Mrs. Maye reads the paper every morning before breakfast, but that particular morning she decided to go to breakfast and read her paper after her meal. On her return from breakfast, she noticed that her paper still had not arrived. "Why haven't I gotten my paper this morning?" she asked one of the CNAs. The CNA replied with an often-heard response, "I will check on it for you." However, the CNA did not follow-up on Mrs. Maye's inquiry; this lack of responsiveness from staff happens often at APAL.

A few CNAs actually try to seek answers for patients when questions arise. When questioned, the CNAs answer in terms of the trade-offs in their positions: "Either we can respond to repeated requests from residents or we can complete our required list of tasks in the stated time. We can't do both!"

Mrs. Maye cannot easily walk to the administrative offices because she often requires help walking or transferring from her rocking chair to her wheelchair; therefore, she rarely sees management to voice her complaints. Each time she pulls her call bell, she is at the mercy of a CNA assigned to her wing of the building, so when she complained about her newspaper, she suspected that her complaint would not be heard. Unless she was able to talk with someone who would be willing to take the problem to management, she thought she might have to give up her morning reading. Rather than give up, however, Mrs. Maye decided she would voice her complaint to everyone with whom she came in contact.

Later that same morning, Bethany King, the medication technician, made her rounds. She noticed a stack of newspapers on the desk next to the nursing station. However, it did not occur to her that residents, including Mrs. Maye, were waiting on the delivery of these papers. When she arrived to Mrs. Maye's room, Mrs. Maye frantically complained that she had not seen the paper yet, and it "was time for her to go to lunch and then to BINGO." Mrs. King, like the CNA, gladly promised Mrs. Maye that she would bring her a newspaper as soon as she saw the last few residents on her schedule.

Mrs. King upheld her promise and delivered a paper to Mrs. Maye an hour later. However, because of her busy schedule, Mrs. King did not say anything to the staff or management about the problem. In fact, she was not even sure whom she should speak to about the issue.

The newspaper continued to be delivered late to Mrs. Maye's room every day during the next two weeks. One afternoon a volunteer delivered mail to Mrs. Maye and heard the story of the late papers.

After leaving Mrs. Maye's room, the volunteer sought the director of activities. The volunteer told the director everything that Mrs. Maye said, including her critical remarks about the three CNAs assigned to her wing.

QUESTIONS FOR DISCUSSION

1. What types of organizational changes need to be made at Aged in Place Assisted Living (APAL) so that Mrs. Maye can voice her complaints to management on a regular basis?
2. Do you think Mrs. Maye's complaint is valid or are there more serious problems?
3. How can management gain the trust of the hourly staff?
4. What are some reasons that APAL might be losing employees regardless of pay?
5. What role could volunteers play in improving resident satisfaction?

PART TWELVE

Organizational Life Cycle

Case 26: Student Coalition for Immigrants and Farmworkers

☐ *Organizational Life Cycle*
◈ *Organizational Structure*
◯ *Migrant Health Network*

FOCUSED TOPIC DESCRIPTION

This case addresses the necessity of organizational change in enabling organizational growth and success.

LEARNING/TEACHING OBJECTIVES

- To understand how organizational change is affected by the organizational life-cycle stage
- To understand the role of resources in determining organizational change

BACKGROUND AND CASE OVERVIEW

Student Coalition for Immigrants and Farmworkers (SCIF) is a young, not-for-profit organization that is building a network of campus-based projects that focus on migrant and seasonal farmworker issues. Based in Durham, North Carolina, these campus-based projects often include both summer internships and year-round opportunities for direct service, community aware-ness, advocacy, and coordination. SCIF also serves as a national internship referral system and an information clearinghouse on farmworker issues. SCIF's mission is to provide services to stu-dents who need assistance in developing quality service-learn-ing programs for farmworkers, who are one of the hardest work-ing, yet most marginalized, groups in American society. SCIF also serves the understaffed agencies and community groups that support farmworkers.

The organization was formed in November 1992 by a recent college graduate, Phil Garcia, who participated in a project simi-lar to those described above during his undergraduate studies. Phil believed that his community service work had greatly en-hanced his college education and leadership skills. He also be-lieved that college students were a wonderful, but often over-looked, resource who could be utilized by overwhelmed agencies that work with marginalized populations in the United States. Phil interviewed many staff members from agencies and univer-sities in North Carolina and found a lack of commitment to ser-vice learning. "I hope that SCIF can fill this gap in the educa-tional system," Phil said regarding this lack of commitment.

ORGANIZATIONAL PROBLEM

During SCIF's first year, Phil allocated fundraising awards to a summer internship program, rather than to his executive direc-tor salary. He raised enough money from private foundations and individual donor solicitations to fund 34 summer interns from North Carolina, South Carolina, Virginia, Tennessee, and California for 10-week internships in North and South Carolina. SCIF's first-year accomplishments were phenomenal, but unfor-tunately these endeavors were achieved at the cost of Phil's time—

he worked an average of 80 hours per week. "I feel so overworked and torn continually among the tasks of fundraising, planning, expansion, and being more involved with the current summer internship program," Phil used to think.

In search of a solution to his frustrating dilemma, Phil sent a grant proposal to The Commission on National and Community Service for a two-year, $135,500 matching grant to fund The Fields, which includes The SCIF Summer Internship and Leadership Development Program. The Leadership Development Program is designed to assist 10 college campuses in North Carolina and South Carolina in developing their own leadership and service programs over a two-year period. Phil wanted to capitalize on the new presidential commitment to community service to bring stable funding and government support to SCIF's growth and success. SCIF was awarded the grant in May 1993. Phil and the SCIF's board of directors were excited about the award and anxiously awaited the implementation of the new program. The organizational changes that resulted from this federal award would begin in September 1993.

The grant provided funding for a full-time project coordinator, which meant that Phil and several board members would have to become more formalized and form a personnel committee responsible for initiating and implementing the addition of a new staff member. By September, the personnel committee recruited nationally for a coordinator, interviewed applicants, and hired Bea Adaul from Michigan. In turn, the personnel committee proposed a new personnel policy, which was approved by the board.

A new matching fund from the federal grant also kept the finance and fundraising committees busy. The grant money required the implementation of an entirely new accounting system, which complicated SCIF's accounting processes. The board of directors recruited an accountant to handle SCIF's accounting responsibilities. The accountant was experienced and good at his job, but believed that allegiance to traditional accounting systems was preeminent. The accountant challenged the fund-raising committee to raise matching funds to support SCIF's rapid growth.

As SCIF continued to grow, it seemed that increased complexity was required to run operations efficiently. Phil now had more help, but in his free hours he wondered if he did not have too much help. He was working fewer hours, but seemed to be fretting more often; at least when he was working so many hours he had everything under control. Now his organization seemed as if it was being pulled in several directions.

QUESTIONS FOR DISCUSSION

1. Why were the organizational changes necessary after Student Coalition for Immigrants and Farmworkers (SCIF) had been so successful in its first year of existence?
2. Describe the situation and conflict in terms of the life-cycle perspective.*
3. Why did Phil run into little, if any, resistance to change?
4. As SCIF grows and progresses through its organizational life cycle, will future changes be implemented successfully?

---

*Life cycle refers to a predictable pattern of change. When applied to organizations, the metaphor suggests that organizations move through stages from birth to growth and expansion to solidification of mission and to eventual decline. The life-cycle stage of an organization is linked to structure and formalization.

PART THIRTEEN

Organizational Size

Case 27: It's Alive!

◻ *Organizational Size*
◇ *Organizational Structure*
◎ *Department of Family Medicine*

FOCUSED TOPIC DESCRIPTION

This case focuses on how an organization's structure must adapt to changes in organizational size.

LEARNING/TEACHING OBJECTIVES

- To understand how a department of a teaching hospital must react to growth to further its mission
- To recognize the dynamic relationship that exists between size and structure
- To be cognizant of the effect of an increase in organizational size on formalization, socialization, and communication

BACKGROUND AND CASE OVERVIEW

The University Family Medical Center (FMC) is a freestanding unit that is part of a teaching medical center and located on the University's greater campus. Attending and resident physicians of the University's School of Medicine staff the FMC. The FMC has a 30-exam room primary care clinic and related laboratory and information systems. The mission of the FMC is to serve the primary needs of the community and to be a training site for residents and medical students, which increases the supply of primary care physicians in the state. The FMC clearly values patient care as well as teaching and research.

Because of the need for healthcare facilities in surrounding rural areas, FMC has opened several satellite clinics. The newest location is in Pilar City and has been having some difficulties adjusting to management directing their activities from another location.

ORGANIZATIONAL PROBLEM

The addition of the clinics to the FMC umbrella increased the total number of employees that management now needed to supervise, which also affected the availability of on-site supervisors. David Blau, FMC's top administrator, wanted an "outsider" to analyze the current situation to determine what changes, if any, needed to be made at the Pilar City clinic. Thus, Jen Isley, the summer intern, was asked to assess the needs of the Pilar City clinic to determine if the expansion required changes to FMC's existing structure.

Mr. Blau called Jen into his office to explain his theory on the subject. "Size is the most important condition affecting the structure of organizations," Mr. Blau stated. But Jen was determined to find out for herself.

Jen found that the Pilar City location strained to operate without an on-site manager. Decisions took a long time to make because they needed the approval of someone who was there only once a week. FMC was growing but the staff at Pilar City felt like it were being stifled. Jen listened to various complaints, including: "Mr. Blau is never here. How can he know what is best for our facility?" and "What exactly does he want to accomplish? We feel like he should give us some guidelines."

After numerous site visits, Jen also found that some employees believed that size did not have a high correlation with an organization's structure. They thought that size was the result, not the cause, of the structural dimensions of the Pilar City facility and that the demands of the environment determined structure, which in turn determined size. Who is right—Mr. Blau or the staff at the Pilar City clinic?

Jen returned to Mr. Blau's office to report her findings. "It's as if it's alive! Our department just seems to keep growing so it could meet the demands of the community," Jen hypothesized. "We need to give our organization all the right things to facilitate this growth. We need to change our structure."

What "things" do you think she was talking about?

QUESTIONS FOR DISCUSSION

1. Discuss how a change in organizational size probably affected University Family Medical Center's (FMC) policies on centralization, formalization, and complexity.
2. If you were the director, how would you have addressed the Pilar City clinic's staff's accusations that you were never there?
3. Should FMC continue to expand in light of the new challenges it will face with each new clinic?

4. Do you agree with Mr. Blau's statement that "size is the most important condition affecting the structure of organizations"?

5. If you were given the same assignment as Jen, what questions would you have asked? Who would you have talked to?

Case 28: Wham! No Standardization

☐ *Organizational Size*
◇ *Organizational Effectiveness*
◎ *State Education Network*

FOCUSED TOPIC DESCRIPTION

This case focuses on the importance and role of formalization in the daily office procedures of health service organizations.

LEARNING/TEACHING OBJECTIVES

- To develop an understanding of how a lack of formalization at the operational level can affect the ability of employees to fulfill their job responsibilities and to further the mission of the organization

BACKGROUND AND CASE OVERVIEW

The Gibson Area Health Education Center (Gibson AHEC) is an affiliate of the Watson University Area Health Education Centers Program and of the Gibson Metropolitan Medical Center (GMMC), a large, urban, tertiary-care facility in the Southeast. Gibson AHEC is physically located within the GMMC campus in the education building. Gibson AHEC provides continuing education services for health and medical care providers, clinical and practical training for health science students and residents, and technical assistance to healthcare-related institutions for manpower and educational issues. Gibson AHEC has a divisional structure with several separate departments; each department has a staff of directors and assistants who are responsible for programs that affect different segments of the population. Because of the linkage between Gibson AHEC and GMMC, the two organizations share many vital administrative services and financial resources; Gibson AHEC is partially funded by the state and by GMMC.

ORGANIZATIONAL PROBLEM

Vicki Colson was recently hired as an assistant in one of the departments at Gibson AHEC. She has been assigned all of the duties previously performed by the continuing education assistant whom she is replacing. Unfortunately, the assistant left no status report that details the timeline of work in progress. Still, when Ms. Colson arrived on the job, she was told to "just get to it." She remembers well her discussion with the director, Alfred Medina.

"Vicki, welcome aboard! We're thrilled to have you. I know that you're eager to get started, so I will not keep you any longer," Mr. Medina quipped enthusiastically. "We're confident in your abilities and we're sure that you will be successful in your new position."

Ms. Colson's first assignment was to prepare a bulk mailing for an upcoming continuing education program. Because the task was too large for her and the hospital mailroom personnel to complete, she had to locate a mailing company to complete the assignment. While waiting to use the copier, she asked her coworkers about the standard bulk mailing protocols within her department. "Mr. Medina asked me to send copies of this brochure to each of the potential program participants, but I'm not sure how to do it. Is there any type of manual I can refer to or is there a particular company that you normally use?"

"No, sorry. I don't know of any manual and I'm not very familiar with that kind of job," replied one of her coworkers. "I work with much smaller groups and I usually do the mailings myself. If I were you, I'd just call around and find the most convenient company. Didn't you attend a training session or get any information from Mr. Medina on what your job covered?"

"No, he's very enthusiastic, but I never received any kind of training. I've already been here over a week and no one has mentioned that possibility either," Ms. Colson admitted.

Ms. Colson continued asking around, but received the same response. Following the advice she was given, she called and identified a company that seemed well suited to her needs. After the brochures were mailed, she received an invoice for the services performed. She gave the invoice to Mr. Medina who then passed it along to the Accounting department for processing and payment. A week later, Accounting returned the invoice to Ms. Colson, refusing to pay it. Apparently, the company Ms. Colson chose was not previously authorized as a vendor for GMMC or its affiliates. Had Vicki requested authorization from the Accounting department prior to the service, an account could have been established with the mailing company. As she had failed to request authorization, the Accounting department refused to make the requested payment. Who will pay the bill and who is responsible for this dilemma?

QUESTIONS FOR DISCUSSION

1. Discuss how formalization in a complex environment, such as at Gibson AHEC-GMMC, played a role in the scenario described.

2. Identify the organizational design modeled by Gibson AHEC. Do you think that this organization uses the most appropriate design option for its operation?
3. If you were faced with this scenario, to whom would you have turned for guidance? What solutions would you suggest?
4. In what ways could Ms. Colson's transition into her new job at Gibson AHEC have been made easier?
5. Relate the problems of this case to others discussed in class. What are some of the consequences, both positive and negative, for Gibson AHEC of the suggestions posed in Question 4?

PART FOURTEEN

Organizational Structure and Design

Case 29: And In This Corner...

☐ *Organizational Structure: Formalization*
◇ *Communication*
◎ *Hospital*

FOCUSED TOPIC DESCRIPTION

This case addresses formalization and how it can positively enhance organizational and employee behavior.

LEARNING/TEACHING OBJECTIVES

- To understand how formalization influences interper-
  sonal relations and communication
- To address the importance of focused job descriptions
  and adequate job training

BACKGROUND AND CASE OVERVIEW

Manilla Hospital is a 152-bed, not-for-profit hospital located in
Reidsville, a small city in the southwest. Manilla is the only
healthcare facility for the surrounding community of 50,000.
Manilla operates inpatient and outpatient facilities, a nursing

care facility, a home health agency, and several specialty clinics. Manilla's Community Services department handles public relations and marketing efforts targeted at the surrounding areas. In addition, Community Services is responsible for volunteer activities, maternal and infant education, and occupational health services.

ORGANIZATIONAL PROBLEM

Last spring, the occupational health coordinator decided to accept a different position within Manilla, which left Community Services to announce the opening and begin conducting interviews. After several weeks of screening potential candidates, the director of Community Services, Anne Foreman, decided that Karen Ali, a recent graduate of a North Carolina university, would be the best fit for the position. Ms. Ali completed a Bachelor of Science degree in occupational health services and was very enthusiastic about this new opportunity. However, at the end of her first week as occupational health coordinator, Ms. Ali still did not have a clear understanding of her responsibilities. She tried to convey her frustrations to Ms. Foreman, who never seemed to have time to answer any questions. Two more weeks passed and Ms. Ali's frustrations continued to build.

One afternoon, Ms. Ali had a pressing question regarding the proper billing procedures for services rendered through her department, so when she spotted Ms. Foreman in the hallway, she began to ask, "Can I ask you a very important...." But before Ms. Ali could finish her question, Ms. Foreman interrupted, "Can't talk now, I'm late for a meeting! Call my secretary. She'll squeeze you in sometime next week."

"Yeah, right," Ms. Ali thought.

Ms. Ali soon came to realize that there was not a clearly stated job description for her position. To complicate the situation, Ms. Ali's dependence on Ms. Foreman for guidance and approval, also known as one-way task dependence, heightened the building frustrations between them. For instance, when Ms. Ali developed ideas of her own to promote occupational health awareness in the community, she needed Ms. Foreman's approval and marketing capabilities to get the program started. Because of organizational protocols, Ms. Ali simply could not move forward without Ms. Foreman's input.

Ms. Foreman began to notice the negative change in Ms. Ali's attitude, but still did not find the time to assist her in her job transition. The former occupational health coordinator had been established in her position before Ms. Foreman was hired as director, so the previous coordinator was independent and fairly self-supervised. Ms. Foreman made an implicit assumption that Ms. Ali would be similarly trained.

QUESTIONS FOR DISCUSSION

1. How would you describe the problem presented in this case? What is the conflict? What factors contribute to the increasing tension?
2. To avoid this type of conflict, what efforts could have been made by Ms. Foreman? Ms. Ali? Others?
3. What elements of Manilla's organizational structure most likely contributed to the conflict?

Case 30: A Neverending Battle

☐ *Organizational Structure: Complexity*
◇ *Decision Making*
○ *Alliance*

FOCUSED TOPIC DESCRIPTION

This case illustrates the difficulties that arise when an alliance has a governing board that consists entirely of chief executive officers.

LEARNING/TEACHING OBJECTIVES

- To learn how high turnover rates among CEOs of organizations that form an alliance can affect the stability of the alliance's governing board
- To discuss possible options for the governance structure of an alliance

BACKGROUND AND CASE OVERVIEW

In 1985, 10 hospitals in western North Carolina formed a voluntary alliance, the Mountain Region Hospital Corporation (MRHC). When MRHC was formed, a governing board was also created, which consists of 10 members — CEOs of the hospitals in the alliance. Although a corporate staff of three is responsible for developing and operating MRHC programs, the majority of the decision making is the responsibility of the governing board.

ORGANIZATIONAL PROBLEM

Over the past four years, five of the 10 hospitals have experienced CEO turnover. A change in the top position not only means transition for the individual organization, but for the governing board of MRHC as well. The largest hospital in MRHC, Cedar View Hospital, has never experienced turnover in the CEO position; Benjamin Butner, CEO of Cedar View, has been with the hospital since it opened 25 years ago. Therefore, he has been a member of the MRHC governing board since its formation in the mid-1980s.

Mr. Butner has always assumed the position of informal leader of MRHC's governing board; therefore, he is usually the first one concerned about losing one board member and gaining another. The constant transition of the board has greatly frustrated him.

Mr. Butner recently found out that Cheryle Manning, the CEO of Rock Top Hospital, which is another MRHC hospital, is leaving Rock Top in three weeks. Upon hearing the news, Mr. Butner called Peggy Haley, who is not only his friend but also the secretary of Richard Rives, another MRHC CEO.

"I assume Richard has heard the news: another CEO gone and another CEO that must learn the ropes," Mr. Butner said to Mrs. Haley.

"How in the world are you ever going to create stability among the board members if you keep losing one and gaining another?" Mrs. Haley confirmed.

Mr. Butner responded with a long sigh and asked with great frustration, "So, Peggy, what does Richard think of all this?"

"Well Ben, he has not really said very much," Mrs. Haley answered. "He briefly mentioned it to me, but said that he had more on his plate to worry about than a governing board full of rookies."

Other CEOs at MRHC were experiencing the same concern about the structure of the board, but seemed to be too busy with their organizations to discuss possible solutions. Most of them have the same attitude as Mr. Rives—just let Benjamin worry about it.

The high rate of board member turnover seems to be a neverending battle that has affected both the board's productivity and effectiveness and morale of its members. It has slowed down the meetings, hindered the amount of goals that the board has been able to accomplish, and decreased the commitment of all board members. Mr. Butner seems to be the only one in charge, even though he is not the only CEO who gains advantages from being part of the alliance. He is not sure how to restore the commitment of the CEO's to the board.

After talking with Mrs. Haley, he exasperatedly exclaimed, "Since when am I the only one responsible for this alliance? No one else seems to even care if we have stability or not. No commitment, no concern! You know what? I'm too busy, too!"

QUESTIONS FOR DISCUSSION

1. Why is a high turnover rate among CEOs a significant problem for the Mountain Region Hospital Corporation (MRHC) alliance?
2. Do you think that having a governing board that consists entirely of CEOs is a good idea? Why or why not?
3. Should MRHC consider other governance structure options? If so, should the MRHC governing board

include physicians, board members from the participating organizations, and/or community members?

4. What are the strengths and weaknesses of having an alliance governing board made up of various representatives such as the members listed in Question 3?

Case 31: A New Male Supervisor

☐ *Organizational Structure: Formalization*
◇ *Conflict*
○ *Diagnostic Center*

FOCUSED TOPIC DESCRIPTION

This case focuses on the reaction of employers to increased formalization of daily office procedures and explores the issue of gender roles.

LEARNING/TEACHING OBJECTIVES

- To develop an understanding of how enacting formalization procedures hastily can cause serious tension and conflict in the work setting
- To explore the role of gender as an underlying cause of organizational conflict

BACKGROUND AND CASE OVERVIEW

The Fayetteville Diagnostic Center (FDC) is a freestanding imaging center located in the Southeast. The FDC offers a full spectrum of over 50 different imaging and outpatient procedures, including MRI and ultrasound. The Fayetteville area is a very transient community because of the large military base located within; however, rural communities surround the area beyond the base. There are three main hospitals in Fayetteville—a community hospital, a private hospital, and a military hospital. The level of managed care penetration is low, but is increasing rapidly.

In the past two years the patient volume at the FDC has more than quadrupled, while employee productivity has not increased because of inefficient, separate employee working systems. This structure was causing a back up of old work and poor results of administrative duties.

ORGANIZATIONAL PROBLEM

The FDC has approximately 55 employees. Except for the administrator, all of the employees are female; most are connected in some way to the military. Consequently, the FDC experiences a yearly employee turnover rate of over 40 percent in all positions, except in upper management positions. Most of the administrative staff duties are clearly identified but job descriptions are flexible and much is left to the discretion of individual employees. This flexibility has allowed employees to develop their own system for completing tasks and job duties.

Robert Reese was recently hired as supervisor to coordinate the duties of 12 employees into one system to increase their productivity; he is the second male employee at the FDC. Mr. Reese immediately began instituting new policies and procedures concerning daily operations and created detailed job descriptions for himself and all 12 employees. Upper management was extremely impressed with his performance, but his employees became increasingly frustrated and angry about the new rigid structure that details how they were to fulfill their duties. Conflict developed between Mr. Reese and his employees, and the employees began to show disrespect toward him.

When Melissa Meadows, a transcriptionist, showed up for work two hours late, Mr. Reese asked, "Is there something wrong? You are two hours late."

"No!" barked Ms. Meadows in response.

"I would appreciate it if you would call next time and let us know you will be late so that we can plan accordingly," Mr. Reese explained.

Ms. Meadows shouted back, "Who do you think you are— telling me what I need to do?"

"I am your supervisor," Mr. Reese replied.

Ms. Meadows stood up and left the room.

At other times when Mr. Reese asked his employees to help with a task, he received no response or a negative remark. For example, one afternoon Mr. Reese received a list of names whose charts needed to be pulled for the next day. "Ernestine, can you please help me pull the charts for tomorrow?" he asked his head file clerk, but received no response.

"Ernestine, I need to pull about one hundred charts. Can you help me, please?" he repeated. She said nothing, stood up from her desk, and walked away without acknowledging Mr. Reese.

Shocked, Mr. Reese walked over to the other file clerk and again asked, "Jill, could you please help me pull these charts for tomorrow?"

"Robert, I'm real busy right now," she replied as she sorts through old chart slips.

"Jill, I really need some help," Mr. Reese pleaded.

"I'm busy sorting these old slips, a task that is specified in my job description," she replied. "Pulling charts is not my job!"

Now very irritated, Mr. Reese snapped, "Yes, it is your job! You work in the file room. Pulling charts is a higher priority task. You can finish sorting those tomorrow. We need to have all the charts pulled by six o'clock tonight."

"Well, you better get started since you only have an hour left," she responded sarcastically.

Mr. Reese's employees do not see him as a supervisor. The atmosphere at the FDC has rapidly become 12 against one. What factors led to the collapse of this department?

QUESTIONS FOR DISCUSSION

1. How was formalization increased? How did it affect this work setting?
2. What could Mr. Reese have done to better motivate his employees to follow a unified system?
3. Given that the staff is all female, does the fact that Mr. Reese is male play a factor in this conflict?
4. Have you ever found yourself in a comparable situation? What were the similarities? Differences? What steps were taken to resolve the situation?

Case 32: Gaining Access to the Hispanic Community

☐ *Organizational Structure: Socialization*
◇ *Environment*
○ *Integrated Care*

FOCUSED TOPIC DESCRIPTION

This case illustrates how differences in socialization among employees can result in organizational conflict.

LEARNING/TEACHING OBJECTIVES

- To understand how socialization of employees can affect reactions to the external environment
- To evaluate how to improve responses to the external environment through increased communication among staff

BACKGROUND AND CASE OVERVIEW

GoodHealth of the Carolinas is a voluntary, not-for-profit integrated healthcare system that provides a full continuum of healthcare services for the people in the central region of South Carolina. GoodHealth is made up of 30 facilities that include Mason Regional Hospital, Collins Memorial Hospital, 15 home health sites, six hospice organizations, five emergency medical technician stations, and two fitness centers. Mason Regional Hospital is the flagship facility and the corporate headquarters; its mission is to be the comprehensive center that meets the healthcare and medical needs of all people in the central region.

Mason Regional Hospital has an outstanding reputation for providing quality services. It was ranked by *Modern Healthcare* magazine as one of the top 100 hospitals in the United States. It is equipped with the latest technology and its physicians have expertise that can accommodate 97 percent of all health problems.

Over the last few years, the Internal Revenue Service has placed increasing pressure on not-for-profit healthcare organizations by questioning their revenues, specifically the amount of free indigent care services they provide to the general public. The CEO, board of directors, and vice presidents of GoodHealth thought it was necessary for the organization to expand its Community Benefit program so that it would not be forced to defend its not-for-profit status. GoodHealth executives wanted to reinvest money back into the organization in a way that would continuously contribute to the community through free services. As a result, the Community Health Services division was formed in the spring of last year and a daughter department, Mobile Health Services, was born six months later.

Mobile Health Services is staffed by three licensed practical nurses and three radiology technicians, and equipped with a 50-

foot long van packed with supplies and equipment for conducting blood pressure, cholesterol, and diabetes checks as well as mammography and prostate screenings. Mobile Health Services, which is directed by Lisa Hooker, director of Community Health, is out in the community six days a week.

ORGANIZATIONAL PROBLEM

In May of the following year, while Mrs. Hooker was reading the Mobile Health Service's reports, she realized that only two of the over-200 screenings done in the van had been received by Hispanic men. She was surprised because she had read a report that stated that South Carolina was one of the five states in the nation with the highest rate of growth of Hispanic residents; so why wasn't this population taking advantage of GoodHealth's free screenings? She later realized that Mobile Health Services was not improving access to preventive healthcare nor were they providing health awareness for the Hispanic community.

Mrs. Hooker asked for approval from her vice president, Tamara Mohr, to hire a Hispanic community development coordinator. Alicia Gomez was hired to identify the communities in which Hispanic people lived and what their needs were and to make contacts in the community to set up screening events. The first blood pressure and diabetes screening in a Hispanic area took place a month after Ms. Gomez's arrival.

Mobile Health Services rumbled up a gravel road onto an open field where a hundred Hispanic women, men, and children awaited. As soon as the nurses could get situated, the men were pushing their way onto the van. They were blurting out "Futbol. Futbol." Mrs. Gomez turned to the nurses and said, "We should let the men go first. They must have a game." After the men were screened one of the nurses said in protest, "We do not work on production, nor on their time. We usually only see 10 people an hour, but over the last two hours we have seen at least 50 people! How are we supposed to counsel these patients if we do not speak their language or at least have enough time to?"

Although the women and children were more patient and gave the nurses a little break, the number of screenings had exceeded all previous community screening events and were wearing out the nurses. Many of the adults came with their entire families and expected their children to receive immunizations, which agitated the situation more.

"This is a screening clinic, not a treatment clinic!" complained one frustrated nurse to another. "We do adult screenings, not prevention services for children. Besides, we don't have the time to treat so many patients! In our training, we were taught that you are only to screen a certain number of patients per hour. If we screen the entire family, we are pushing ourselves to provide less than quality medicine."

It was getting late and as the last woman was waiting for her blood pressure results and the nurses were beginning to clean up. Mrs. Gomez opened the van door and began helping the children onto the van. One of the nurses shouted, "Don't you know that we cannot screen children? Our licenses are at stake! The van's policies limit us to adults!"

"I didn't know that you can't screen children. I have told these people that this was ok from the very beginning and that's the most important thing to them!" Mrs. Gomez countered. "If I lose this, then I won't be able to plan anymore events in this area."

The nurses and Mrs. Gomez just stood there exasperated and motionless.

"We can't call Lisa; she's on vacation. But can't you do something?" Mrs. Gomez offered.

One of the nurses glared at her and said, "I'm not in a position that's worth jeopardizing my license for."

QUESTIONS FOR DISCUSSION

1. What problem is presented in this case?
2. Do you think that changes in formalization could have prevented this problem?
3. With Mrs. Gomez being a new employee, could the nurses have helped her out by performing environmental scanning?
4. How would you resolve this crisis?

Case 33: Family Matters at Cariño

☐ *Organizational Structure: Complexity*
◇ *Organizational Change*
◯ *Integrated Care System*

FOCUSED TOPIC DESCRIPTION

This case illustrates how changes and growth in a family business can sometimes lead to placement of family members in strategic positions for which they are not professionally trained.

LEARNING/TEACHING OBJECTIVES

- To understand the difficulties and complications that may arise in a growing family-run healthcare network
- To discover how changes in an organization's structure can affect the customers' perceptions of a healthcare system
- To explore how small proprietorships can implement new organizational structures

173

Cariño Healthcare is an integrated healthcare delivery system that is owned and operated by a Mexican-American family in a small rural community near the Texas/Mexico border. Eduardo Gonzalez founded Cariño 30 years ago as an assisted living center for the elderly. The Center has now grown to include three skilled nursing facilities, four assisted living centers, a pharmacy, and a sales division for durable medical equipment. Much of the growth has occurred during the past 10 years when patients were leaving hospitals more quickly but required more transitional care. Cariño, which operated on a $2 million budget in 1998, now operates on a $50 million budget. Cariño has been quite successful because it has a good reputation for providing quality care and because the owner and his family are part of the local Mexican-American community.

ORGANIZATIONAL PROBLEM

Mr. Gonzalez is getting older and is ready to retire. He would like to have his sons, who range in age from 22 to 29, serve as the managers of his enterprise. The oldest of the three sons has a bachelor's degree in pharmacy, but is currently away attending medical school; the middle son started college, but only completed one semester before returning home to work for his father; the youngest son has a bachelor's degree in industrial engineering.

Because Cariño has grown so quickly and has opened so many additional facilities, the middle and youngest sons have had a difficult time managing the organization and have not been accepting management duties responsibly—they take more days off than other employees; they come in late; they leave early; and they graciously accept all the company perks, such as samples and gifts offered by suppliers and sales representatives. By their behavior, it is evident that the company's mission is not their top priority. Seeing this, Mr. Gonzalez has not been comfortable with retirement and does not know where to turn next.

The behavior of Mr. Gonzalez's sons is predictable given the organization's historical structure. For almost three decades, Mr. Gonzalez has operated Cariño and made all of the key decisions on his own—everyone went to him with problems and he provided solutions—but now Cariño has become too complex an operation for only one person to manage. The simple organizational structure that once existed at Cariño is now obsolete and, clearly, a more divisional structure is needed. However, that will require hiring outside the family, even if Mr. Gonzalez chooses to wait for his eldest son to return after completing medical school.

The formal lines of communication and channels for decision making at Cariño are unclear because they are new and sometimes uncomfortable. Furthermore, in the past, job descriptions were very general in nature or did not exist because the company was simple and operations were informal because of the extended family nature of the business. However, Cariño is now at a critical juncture: it has maximized its market share in the local community and its services continue to expand. As services continue to expand, opportunities to form partnerships and allies multiply, as well. Recently, Cariño was given the opportunity to help a much larger healthcare organization develop primary care facilities in the same town. This development would bring new referrals to Cariño and give it a chance to expand geographically with the larger institution.

In addition, Carson Memorial Hospital, the local hospital in the community, recently formed an alliance and is currently seeking a home health agency in the area to join the alliance. Carson Memorial Hospital also has the desire to reach the minority community in the county, so it is highly likely that Cariño will be asked to join the alliance.

As Cariño's structure becomes increasingly complex and the external environment continues to provide opportunity for growth, it is imperative that Cariño hire responsible people for strategic positions so that decisions made are positive and effective. Mr. Gonzalez sees the opportunities, but knows he should retire. He is troubled and uncertain about his next steps.

QUESTIONS FOR DISCUSSION

1. In your opinion, should Mr. Gonzalez allow his sons to take over as managers or find other, more qualified administrators? Why?
2. If Mr. Gonzales decides to allow his sons to run Cariño, how could he motivate them to improve their performance and commitment?
3. What effects might changes in administration have on employee morale at Cariño? on the customer's perception of Cariño?
4. Should Cariño remain a proprietorship or move to a corporate alliance model? What are the advantages and disadvantages of each strategy?

Case 34: "I Can't Do It All!"

☐ *Organizational Structure: Centralization*
◇ *Leadership*
◎ *Health Maintenance Organization*

FOCUSED TOPIC DESCRIPTION

This case addresses how a highly centralized structure contributes to staff problems within the strategic apex of Healthdyne organization.

LEARNING/TEACHING OBJECTIVES

- To learn the advantages and disadvantages of high versus low centralization
- To discuss effective methods for communication and delegation
- To identify challenges of changing leadership styles

BACKGROUND AND CASE OVERVIEW

Based in Walnut Creek, California, Healthdyne is a health maintenance organization (HMO) that provides healthcare to the northern California bay area. It serves approximately 1.2 million enrollees composed mainly of upper class, white-collar professionals. Healthdyne occupies a relatively small corner of the market, but is quickly gaining prominence in the area and has developed a solid financial footing with bright prospects. It is located in a growing community, with a 15 to 20 percent annual growth rate projected for the next five years.

For the past 20 years, Healthdyne's former president, Amanda Huggins, has successfully carried out the organizational mission—to provide more affordable and better quality healthcare for its members by setting the statewide standard for excellence and responsiveness. As one of the key players in the organization since its inception, Ms. Huggins is a recognized expert in the managed care industry. Corporate legend has it that her motto was "It doesn't happen without my signature!" Upon Ms. Huggins's retirement, Arnold Brice was recruited to take her place.

ORGANIZATIONAL PROBLEM

When Mr. Brice, who is the former CEO of Atlantic Healthcare, was brought in as president, he inherited an executive staff composed of vice presidents of Marketing, Finance, and Professional Services departments as well as a medical director, all of whom were capable of fulfilling their managerial responsibilities. However, within a few weeks of joining Healthdyne, Mr. Brice perceived a serious flaw with his staff—none of the vice presidents would make a decision, not even on routine matters such as personnel questions, choice of marketing media, or changing suppliers. The vice presidents frequently presented him with issues in their areas of responsibility and requested that he make the decision. This troubled Mr. Brice. Before long, the situation seriously impeded his efforts to engage in strategic planning for the HMO.

At a regular staff meeting, when every member of his staff had an issue that required his attention, Mr. Brice finally blew up. The catalyst to this incident was this question from the Finance vice president: "What font do you want this in?"

Waving his arms in exasperation, Mr. Brice shouted, which is very uncharacteristic of him, "I cannot do it all! You are going to have to make these decisions yourselves."

The meeting broke up with the staff looking very puzzled, and Mr. Brice realizing that he had to make serious changes.

QUESTIONS FOR DISCUSSION

1. What is the main conflict present at Healthdyne?
2. What organizational structures and/or individuals contributed to this problem?
3. If Healthdyne had continued to be run in this manner, what are some possible consequences for a) staff relations and morale and b) organizational productivity and efficiency?
4. Compare and contrast the advantages and disadvantages of each president's leadership style.
5. Suggest tactics to initiate change. What ends do you hope to achieve?
6. How does the centralized structure of Healthdyne affect the way employees interact and behave?

Case 35: Who's the Boss?

☐ *Organizational Structure: Complexity*
◇ *Communication*
◎ *Teaching Hospital*

FOCUSED TOPIC DESCRIPTION

This case illustrates the importance of establishing open channels of communication between employees and their supervisors when utilizing certain organizational designs.

LEARNING/TEACHING OBJECTIVES

- To recognize the importance of matching the proper organizational design model with institution-wide projects
- To demonstrate the necessity of increased communication between employees and their supervisors when utilizing a matrix organizational design
- To expose the weaknesses of certain organizational design strategies

BACKGROUND AND CASE OVERVIEW

The University Medical Center (UMC) is a 670-bed academic medical center and teaching institution. Centrally located in Iowa City, Iowa, UMC serves patients from each of the state's 99 counties and beyond. UMC admits approximately 25,000 inpatients each year, and 500,000 outpatients are seen annually in UMC's related comprehensive clinics. Overall, UMC supports 650 faculty participants in over 50 medical specialties. As in many academic teaching institutions, UMC structures clinical administration around the medical school's teaching departments. For example, each medical department administers certain clinics, while UMC's Outpatient Administration sets policies and facilitates coordination among the various clinical departments.

In recent years, Outpatient Administration has been contemplating the redesign of its communication center through the purchase of a centralized calling center. If the centralized center were implemented, patients would be able to call one central telephone number when requesting information or scheduling appointments. This design has the potential to drastically reduce patient confusion and streamline lengthy information-collection procedures. Currently, to make an appointment at UMC, a patient must call the proper secretary within a specific medical school department. If the patient has not previously been seen at UMC, he/she must also call a separate registration number to provide needed insurance information.

ORGANIZATIONAL PROBLEM

To move one step closer to a centralized calling center, Outpatient Administration recently approved a pilot project to study the effects of requesting insurance information at the time an appointment is made. While this change is easier for patients at the front end, it is unknown whether or not UMC's information systems can effectively centralize for billing purposes. There is the possibility that patients will have to repeat the information at the time of their appointment. UMC's Continuous Quality Improvement (CQI) department is leading the project, and it assigned Lisa Starring as the project team leader. Because the project is a pilot, CQI has asked employees from different functional departments to meet to form the Project Team.

Dr. Patrick Hanley, the ambitious newly appointed director of Medicine, enthusiastically volunteered the Pulmonary Clinic within his department to participate in the Project Team's upcoming pilot. Dr. Hanley sent a memorandum to the manager of the Pulmonary Clinic, Shirley Middleton, that requests that she "provide the use of Jerry Douglas, administrative support officer, for the upcoming CQI pilot project."

Jerry Douglas, an extremely diligent worker, currently shuffles the Pulmonary Clinic's scheduling processes with the rest of his duties. Jerry's current primary project is a challenging clinical-performance assessment tool for Ms. Middleton. As a result of his added CQI responsibility, he will now be reporting to both Ms. Middleton and Ms. Starring.

When Ms. Middleton informed Jerry of his appointment to the Project Team in the upcoming months, she also covertly reminded him of his project for her: "I can't wait for the unveiling of your assessment tool next month, Jerry."

Following initial planning meetings, the CQI Project Team began pre-registering Pulmonary Clinic patients at the time of the appointment call. Ms. Starring made numerous contacts with Jerry throughout the workday to examine the project's progress. Jerry found that instead of the usual two to three hours he spends on scheduling patients, he was now spending close to six to eight hours scheduling and registering individuals for visits to the Pulmonary Clinic. As a result of his work overload, he was forced to spend hours and hours of personal time to catch up on his clinical-performance assessment tool project.

Overwhelmed and exhausted, Jerry scheduled a meeting with Ms. Middleton and Ms. Starring. "I simply cannot register patients the entire day and keep up with my other duties," Jerry complained. "I'm supposed to present my performance assessment tool in front of the entire Medicine department in two days and I'm weeks behind on the work!"

"You're what?!" Ms. Middleton screamed. "I'm counting on you to deliver that presentation, Jerry!"

"Excuse me, but the Project Team has much more important data to collect. I hope you're not implying that you intend to abort the project," interrupted Ms. Starring. "We've already invested our time in you and have the grace of Dr. Hanley to use you at our discretion."

"Who do you think you are, Lisa?" Ms. Middleton countered. "Jerry is my employee and he will place my deadline over your work."

"Shirley, I don't think you understand," replied Lisa. "CQI's work takes precedent over measly projects such as yours. Jerry will answer to me!"

"Now, I'm nobody's employee!" Jerry shouted in exasperation. He stood up and left the room forever.

QUESTIONS FOR DISCUSSION

1. What was the primary source of the conflict among Jerry, Ms. Middleton, and Ms. Starring? Why? What factors at University Medical Center (UMC) led to this conflict?
2. Could Jerry's departure been prevented? What roles should have been taken by each of the parties above to prevent this conflict?

3. List the strengths and weaknesses of using a matrix model in this case.
4. Which organizational design option, if any, offers an alternative to use as a matrix model for this communication-oriented pilot project?

Case 36: Keeping Spirits High

☐ *Organizational Structure: Centralization*
◇ *Motivation*
◯ *Hospital*

FOCUSED TOPIC DESCRIPTION

This case showcases the effect of centralized decision making on employee motivation, morale, performance, and efficiency within a dynamic environment.

LEARNING/TEACHING OBJECTIVES

- To learn how centralization affects employee morale, performance, and efficiency
- To assess the benefits and risks of centralization versus decentralization

BACKGROUND AND CASE OVERVIEW

Metro Care Hospital is a for-profit teaching hospital that serves a large population ranging from the area's wealthiest to the area's most indigent. It is located in the heart of a metropolitan area and is flanked by two nationally acclaimed teaching facilities. Metro Care is known for its excellent primary and specialty care services and at times receives up to 3,000 referrals in a single day. On average, Metro Care serves approximately 10,000 to 15,000 patients daily.

The Cost Accounting department is one of many departments located within the Metro Care health system. Its main objective is to compile and report all Medicare reimbursable services provided by any of the hospital's 300 patient care departments to Dr. Douglas Knowel, the executive director of Metro Care. Dr. Knowel, in turn, reports the Medicare cost report findings to the board of directors. Recognizing the amount of time and research necessary to complete the Medicare cost report, Cost Accounting employs five full-time staff members—a director, two assistant directors, and two clerical/research positions. Funds to staff two additional part-time clerks are available, but the positions are not always filled.

ORGANIZATIONAL PROBLEM

For the past 10 years, the Medicare cost report had been due on December 31, six months after the closing of Metro Care's fiscal year on June 30. Lauren Dobbins, the director of Cost Accounting, had assumed complete responsibility for the production and accuracy of the report in the past. However, now she increasingly spends much of her time in meetings. On an average day, Ms. Dobbins spends up to five hours in meetings at the hospital and at nearby agencies and an additional two hours traveling back and forth. Because of her limited time schedule, she has delegated the majority of the responsibility of the Medicare cost report to other departmental staff members. However, she still insists on complete authority when it comes to decision making. She determines who is responsible for preparing certain aspects of the report, how the sections are written, what information needs to be included or excluded, and how the final report should be presented. "I may not have time to complete the entire project, but I'll be damned if it is not done the way I want! My job is riding on the accuracy and appearance of this report," she has been known to have said once.

At the end of the current fiscal year, Dr. Knowel met with Ms. Dobbins to discuss her department's responsibilities. "Because of the way you have successfully handled the Medicare cost report in the past, I have assigned your department two additional projects," Dr. Knowel told Ms. Dobbins. Ms. Dobbins was excited to learn the new responsibilities, but her spirits were dampened when Dr. Knowel informed her that the deadline for this year's Medicare cost report would be moved up from December 31 to September 30. Ms. Dobbins knew that this would be a sensitive subject to relay to her staff, particularly the two clerks/researchers. Most of the work for the report was done by these two staff members, while the two higher-paid assistant directors constantly submitted revisions to Ms. Dobbins for approval. Mr. Strayhorn, an assistant director, complained about his lack of responsibility: "Given my extensive training and my intellect, I should be responsible for projects that require more higher-level thinking."

At the first departmental meeting for the new fiscal year, Ms. Dobbins, without prior warning, informed the Cost Accounting staff that the deadline for the Medicare cost report had been moved up to September 30. In essence, the staff now only had three months to prepare the report, as opposed to six. Before excusing herself to attend an executive meeting, Ms. Dobbins remarked, "I know we all have our problems with this arrangement, but if everyone doesn't complain and does their own work efficiently, we'll all keep our jobs."

One month after the end of the fiscal year, Dr. Knowel visited Cost Accounting to assess the progress that had been made on the Medicare cost report. Not surprisingly, Ms. Dobbins was out of town attending a national Medicare financing conference and was not scheduled to return until next week. Instead of optimum efficiency, Dr. Knowel discovered that not only had two employees resigned, but the remaining workers were bickering about the scope of their individual responsibilities. Worse still, the department was at serious risk of not completing the report by the new deadline. He was extremely upset and disillusioned with Ms. Dobbins's lack of ability to delegate responsibility and provide clear individual and team direction to all staff. Based on his assumption that all was well in Ms. Dobbins's department, Dr. Knowel had gone through great efforts to schedule and prepare a year-end presentation for the upcoming board of directors meeting. Dr. Knowel had anticipated bragging about Metro Care's 23 percent increase in profits.

QUESTIONS FOR DISCUSSION

1. In your opinion, what appears to be the root of Cost Accounting's problems?
2. What immediate suggestions would you make for reorganizing Cost Accounting?
3. What changes do you suggest to improve employee morale, performance, and efficiency?

PART FIFTEEN

Power, Control, and Politics

Case 37: CFO versus CEO

☐ *Power and Control*
◇ *Decision Making*
◎ *Community Hospital*

FOCUSED TOPIC DESCRIPTION

This case describes how centralized authority can blur the distinction between power and control when decisions are made in a small rural hospital.

LEARNING/TEACHING OBJECTIVES

- To understand the relationship among centralization, power, and control in an organization
- To realize how lack of understanding of the differences between power and control affect communication, which can hinder effective decision making
- To explore ways to promote and maintain more effective decision making in a highly centralized organization

BACKGROUND AND CASE OVERVIEW

River City Hospital (RCH), a not-for-profit, primary care, medical facility located in rural eastern North Carolina, has been feeling increased pressure to expand their services so as to maintain a competitive edge in the market. A year ago, a large tertiary care teaching hospital—Emerald City Medical Center (ECMC)—located 20 miles away, gained private status. ECMC used this new status to its advantage and quickly purchased several smaller hospitals in the same area, which expanded its service boundaries. ECMC's service population moved closer to RCH's boundaries and, as a result, absorbed a number of potential patients from the area that RCH had considered its secondary service area.

In years past, RCH had seen no need for radical change in the healthcare services it provided nor did it see a need to expand beyond its 140-bed facility. RCH had served the city and surrounding communities quite well, but as ECMC continued to grow larger and more powerful, RCH realized that it had to grow as well so as not to be eclipsed. After a six-month environmental review, RCH's board of trustees approved a $14 million renovation and expansion project. They also encouraged RCH's executive director, Reginald Lipinski, to pursue the acquisition of other health facilities, including a primary care site, a nursing home, and two small home health agencies in the area. Shortly thereafter, RCH purchased one home health agency and an OB/GYN clinic located outside the area.

RCH has been characterized by highly centralized management. For over 20 years, the central authority figures have been the same executive director and chief financial officer. These two authority figures have become readily accustomed to overseeing all organizational decision making and have become so familiar and comfortable with each other's styles that sometimes they seem to intuit, rather than discuss, each other's decisions.

For many years, internal and external operations at RCH were virtually unchanged. In other words, discussions concerning *all* matters were brought to both the CEO and the CFO for approval. But the proposed renovation project and other measures of expansion at RCH, including the purchase of two new facilities, now pose an unexpected threat to this accepted pattern of control.

ORGANIZATIONAL PROBLEM

As an additional part of their expansion, RCH planned to open an Ear, Nose, and Throat (ENT) specialty clinic. A former physician practice office, located beside RCH, was purchased to house the new ENT clinic, but major renovations were needed before it could open. All renovating and decorating for the hospital's satellite clinics are the responsibility of Nancy May, director of Renovation and Interior Design. Like other divisional directors at RCH, Mrs. May was required to seek approval from both the CEO and CFO, so she had to consult with them about redesigning the ENT clinic. She inquired about which plumbers, electricians, and carpenters to contract with; which equipment companies to purchase the specialty equipment from; and how the floor plan of the clinic was to be laid out.

Mrs. May found herself constantly running back and forth between the two men. Despite the complexity of the ENT renovations, the CEO was concerned with opening the clinic as quickly as possible, even if it meant paying overtime for the workmen to come in on weekends. The CFO, on the other hand, was even more concerned with saving money and did not agree with paying the carpenters to work extra hours. Despite these differences, the building renovation continued.

A month before the scheduled opening, Mrs. May approached the CEO to discuss ordering furniture, window treatments, and throw rugs for the waiting area. As he rushed off to an executive meeting, the CEO told her, "Let's go ahead and wrap this project up because I want Dr. Coleman practicing by the end of the month. I play golf with him every Wednesday and I assured him we would have things squared away by then. Order whatever you think is appropriate!" Knowing the furniture would take at least three weeks to arrive and that the CFO was on a two-week vacation, Mrs. May placed her order.

Everything arrived on schedule and just days before opening the clinic, Mrs. May took the purchase order to the CFO's office for his signature. When he saw the total of the bill, he was furious! The following dialogue is an excerpt of that conversation.

CFO: "Nancy, how dare you spend this atrocious amount of money without getting my approval first! What in the world made you buy waiting room furniture that's covered in Ralph Lauren fabrics? Have you lost your mind? You will have to send it all back! I don't care how long it takes to find furniture for that office, but it will not open until you do!"

Mrs. May: "I hope you understand that because of our deadline I needed to go ahead and order the furniture. You were out on vacation when I placed the order so I couldn't get your approval! The CEO said it was fine. He just wanted the clinic to be opened by the end of the month. I simply assumed that you both discussed this issue *before* I asked his approval."

CFO: "Well we *hadn't* discussed it and I *don't* understand that you needed to place the order. Doesn't my approval matter to you? It's my signature that is on the bottom line of all checks written for this hospital!"

It was obvious to Mrs. May that she was caught in the middle of a large power struggle between the two men who tugged at the reigns of RCH. She decided that the next clinic RCH opened would have to be refurbished by someone else.

QUESTIONS FOR DISCUSSION

1. How does centralized authority contribute to power and control struggles and compromise organizational effectiveness?
2. What are some short-term and long-term goals for eliminating problems with decision making at River City Hospital (RCH)?
3. What role does formalization play at RCH given the information in this case?

Case 38: What Went Wrong?

☐ *Power and Control*
◇ *Leadership*
○ *County Health Department*

FOCUSED TOPIC DESCRIPTION

This case presents the negative effects of a *laissez-faire* leadership style.

LEARNING/TEACHING OBJECTIVES

- To identify the characteristics of a *laissez-faire* leadership style
- To distinguish the negative and positive aspects of a *laissez-faire* leadership style

BACKGROUND AND CASE OVERVIEW

New Hampshire County has five to seven small public health facilities that primarily focus on a specific need of a specific population. The New Hanover County Health Department (NHCD), located in the county's principal city, is mandated to provide all aspects of public health services and is the only facility that is available to all residents of the county. In addition, NHCD has two hospitals—a private and a public—a number of physician practices, several home health agencies, and nursing homes.

ORGANIZATIONAL PROBLEM

NHCD is located in a port city along the southern Atlantic coast. The county itself is home to 120,000 residents and its principal city has a population of 80,000. The county has been growing steadily over the years with a large number of people moving from the northeast and a rapid increase in the number of Spanish-speaking immigrants. The influx of new populations has increased the demand for public health services within the county. While there are a handful of public health–oriented facilities within both the city and the county, NHCD is the largest single provider of these healthcare services.

NHCD is composed of eleven divisions including the Communicable Disease Division (CDD). The goal of CDD is to screen, treat, and prevent the spread of infectious diseases including sexually transmitted diseases, HIV/AIDS, and tuberculosis. Susie Toms, a classic *laissez-faire* type leader, is director of CDD. As a manager, Ms. Toms expects her employees to be independent, self-motivated individuals, and she believes that it is an insult to her employees to concern herself with autonomous daily activities; however, she still expects to be consulted when a problem arises. An employee at CDD could go a number of days without an encounter with Ms. Toms if all is going well in his/her work because Ms. Toms does not believe in "interfering" with her employees' work by checking on them. She is convinced that she has hired only the best individuals who always work to their highest potential. And, she believes that with this highly qualified staff, current job descriptions, adjustments in divisional roles and responsibilities, and interim planning meetings are unimportant because everyone knows what is expected of them.

Until recently, Ms. Toms's management philosophy has been highly effective and her staff has produced some of the highest quality work of all the divisions within NHCD. However, in the past few months, one staff member, Emma Sage, has begun to shirk her responsibility, which has increased the workload of other staff members at CDD. In the month of July alone, Mrs. Sage, the HIV team coordinator, pressured a fellow employee into preparing all of the necessary materials for an educational workshop she was teaching because she explained that she was computer illiterate. She also assigned to another coworker the full responsibility for developing and constructing a display board for an HIV conference without offering assistance because she was "too busy." Both coworkers were more than happy to help Mrs. Sage until they learned that she had been "organizing" her office while they were doing these tasks.

When the news of this behavior hit Ms. Toms's office, she was both shocked and disappointed. She always had the utmost confidence in Mrs. Sage's capabilities, but was concerned at the laziness that she was exhibiting. Ms. Toms was also aware that she must first change her approach to influence the change in Mrs. Sage's behavior and attitude. Ms. Toms pondered how Mrs. Sage's attitude had reached this uncaring point and what changes she could make to rectify the situation.

QUESTIONS FOR DISCUSSION

1. What is the primary source of this conflict? Why?
2. What characteristics of Ms. Toms's leadership style promoted Mrs. Sage's behavior?
3. What are some of the ways that Ms. Toms could alter her management style to prevent this type of behavior from reoccurring?

PART SIXTEEN

Technology

Case 39: A Double Standard

☐ *Technology*
◇ *Communication*
◎ *Physician Practice*

FOCUSED TOPIC DESCRIPTION

This case focuses on how technology improves organizational communication.

LEARNING/TEACHING OBJECTIVES

- To assess the potential benefits of using modern technology to improve communication within an organization
- To assess how the lack of technology can harm an organization's effectiveness
- To identify options for finding a compromise between keeping the costs of technology low and maintaining patient satisfaction

BACKGROUND AND CASE OVERVIEW

Stanton Memorial Hospital, a 247-bed private hospital, is one of two not-for-profit community hospitals in Rural Heights, North Carolina. The hospital has a very positive reputation because of its long-standing commitment to providing quality healthcare at a reasonable cost. Some examples of this commitment include the CEO's, Harry Cummings, involvement with patient feedback reports, charitable community activities, and affordable healthcare in the area. Because of Stanton's commitment to providing quality healthcare at the lowest possible price, Mr. Cummings insists on buying only what is absolutely needed. In fact, from 1993 to 1998, the hospital did not implement any rate increases.

At the same time, however, technology at Stanton is well behind in comparison with the current standard of any healthcare facility. Stanton employees do not have access to voicemail or electronic mail and there is no hospital-wide access to the Internet. The lack of updated technology has a direct influence on internal and external communication methods of the hospital. For example, because the COO, Clay Melvin, is rarely available for walk-in visits, it becomes necessary to phone him if his assistance is needed. However, this method of contact is futile when Mr. Melvin is in meetings, so secretaries must be relied upon to relay numerous messages.

In addition, as the Internet expands in usefulness and importance, its necessity has also become more apparent at Stanton; its personnel continuously look for ways to improve hospital efficiency through use of new products. However, Stanton currently only has one computer with Internet access, so, clearly, its use among the hospital's 850 employees is severely restricted.

ORGANIZATIONAL PROBLEM

During a recent weekly department head meeting, Mr. Cummings asked if there was anything the senior staff would like to discuss. Jeff Morrow, director of the Dietary department, quickly raised his hand and said, "I think we ought to do something about the technology around here. I mean, you want me to provide the best meals available which means keeping the food hot.

Without ready Internet access, I don't really have time to research options for keeping the food warm."

"I agree; do you know how much easier our orders could be if we were hooked up to the Internet?" seconded Mark Sasser, director of the Materials Management department. "I could possibly reduce our shipment time by half!"

Soon, all of the department heads joined in, each pointing out the advantage of updated use of technology in their respective departments. Becoming irate, Mr. Cummings stood up, "Look, can I get your input one at a time, please?" Just then chief ER nurse, Ellen Hatfield spoke and said, "Harry, in addition to Internet access, we really need to do something about our communication within the hospital. We don't have e-mail or voicemail to contact coworkers within the hospital. Clay is so busy that it took him five days by telephone to answer my simple yes or no question, which could have been answered in five seconds if we had e-mail."

"Look, you all agreed that you want this hospital to provide quality, affordable healthcare to our patients. This means reducing unnecessary expenses and eliminating frivolous ones, including technology. We have provided care to date without these devices. The added expense would have to be passed along to our customers," Mr. Cummings pointed out as he stood from the table. "I am not convinced. You have all performed fine without all of these e-mail, voicemail, and Internet devices! You are all thinking about yourselves. I, for one, want to keep my promise to patients. I refuse to hear any more nonsense about incurring useless expenses for technology. This meeting is dismissed!"

QUESTIONS FOR DISCUSSION

1. Is the idea of bringing in all of the new technology (i.e., voicemail, e-mail, and Internet access) a reasonable idea for Stanton? Why or why not?

2. What methods could be used to address the needs of the department heads?
3. How could Mr. Cummings and the department heads reach a compromise that would create favorable outcomes for both parties?
4. Is Mr. Cummings' commitment to patient satisfaction in the best interest of both employees and patients at Stanton? Why or why not?

Case 40: We're Not Gonna Take It Anymore

☐ *Technology*
◇ *Communication*
◎ *Network of Affiliates*

FOCUSED TOPIC DESCRIPTION

This case argues that the increased complexity—geographic differentiation—of a nationwide affiliate network creates a need for upgraded technology that would improve effective organizational communication.

LEARNING/TEACHING OBJECTIVES

- To explore the effect of technological limitations on communication
- To understand the relationship between organizational structure and effective channels of communication
- To identify effective ways for disseminating information in a spatially differentiated environment

BACKGROUND AND CASE OVERVIEW

The Asthma-Free America Network (AFAN) is a private, not-for-profit health service foundation, with a national office located in San Francisco, CA, dedicated to finding a cure for and controlling asthma and allergic diseases, which affect an estimated 50 million Americans. AFAN fulfills its mission through many various activities—patient and public education, public awareness and information, research, patient advocacy, and support of a nationwide network of 13 regional affiliates and over 170 support groups.

Several years ago, AFAN was an obscure organization on the brink of bankruptcy. However, under the leadership of its new executive director, Dr. Pat Wirth, AFAN began its upward climb and is now nationally regarded as an expert in the field of asthma and allergic diseases. Given its scientific and policy expertise, AFAN's staff members are frequently called upon to serve on national advisory panels and to offer testimony in the development of practice guidelines and quality measures.

ORGANIZATIONAL PROBLEM

The AFAN's Annual Executive Directors' Conference, held at the San Francisco office, is the only time during the year when leaders of the regional affiliates come together as one body. This year, very few of the 13 executive directors have spoken with one another, and only about half are aware that four new executive directors had been hired during the past year. The lack of information dissemination is primarily because of the distance that separated the affiliates. Situated in different locations throughout the country, each affiliate has become accustomed to operating like an independent organization. Even Dr. Wirth had only visited nine of the affiliate offices.

Because the AFAN Affiliate Network is so regionally dispersed, there are frequent concerns about what and how information should be exchanged between the national office and the affiliates and among the affiliates. The traditional mail delivery system is still the principal means of communication because most affiliates have limited technologies available to them. While the national office has e-mail and fax capabilities, this is not the case at the majority of affiliate offices. As a result, reviewing documents that require a quick turnaround is very difficult for affiliates with only telephone capability. Furthermore, maintaining correspondence with the affiliates is such a time-consuming activity that the national office staff cannot handle it efficiently. Jamie Allen, director of Finance at the national office, complained, "I don't have the time to deal with each affiliate over every issue and I'm sick of explaining the same issue five times to five different affiliates." As a result, many issues never reach the attention of the affiliate leaders. Decisions are made in the national office without affiliate input and then simply communicated to the affiliates.

Kevin Kilpatrick, the executive director of AFAN's Florida affiliate, is known for his diplomatic style but was quickly losing patience about the way information is shared. "Affiliates are the backbone of this organization!" he reiterated to the attendees. "We are the ones who are out in the community, putting on the programs, and interacting with the patients. We have a right to know what is going on! You can't just lead us along like we are children."

In response to Mr. Kilpatrick's outburst, Dr. Wirth responded, "We simply do not have the time or energy to consult each of you on every issue. If the national office had to correspond with you on everything, we would spend all our time sending you information and no time doing our jobs."

To further compound the problem, the affiliates are discovering that they are duplicating efforts and resources that could have easily been shared. For example, the St. Louis affiliate had spent considerable time and energy developing an asthma education brochure designed for the adolescent population, only to discover later that the Washington office had been pursuing the same thing. Had the two affiliates been in contact, they could have combined their efforts. "If I would have known about those brochures," claimed Tammy Manning from the New England office, "we could have distributed them at the health fairs we organized."

"What do you want us to do?" asked Dr. Wirth.

"We want you to keep us informed of issues as they are happening—not after the fact. Feedback is important," responded Mr. Kilpatrick.

"I agree! national office should help us communicate with each other," said Cheryl McDonald from the Washington office. "We could all save a lot of time and energy by working together and sharing our resources."

"I think that we're all very separated from the national office. Don't forget that our role as affiliates is vital to AFAN's success!" remarked Dave Upshaw of from the Michigan office.

Overcome by frustration, Dr. Wirth finally interrupted, "These are all great ideas, but does anyone have any suggestions for how to make these recommendations come about?"

"I don't know, but you had better do something soon," replied Ms. Manning. "We're tired of not knowing what's going on, and we're not gonna take it anymore!"

QUESTIONS FOR DISCUSSION

1. Determine the primary and secondary issues in the case. What role does technology play as a contributing factor to the Asthma-Free America Network (AFAN) conflict?
2. How do these contributing factors affect the behavior of AFAN's affiliate leadership?
3. Suggest measures that could be taken to resolve the conflict.

About the Authors

DEBORAH E. BENDER, PH.D., MPH, is a professor in the Department of Health Policy and Administration, School of Public Health, at the University of North Carolina at Chapel Hill. She is also the director of the Bachelor of Science Program in Public Health in the Department.

Her career spans 20 years and four continents. She has worked extensively with health services agencies in the United States and in developing countries in South America, Africa, and Asia. The focus of her work is on the improvement of quality of health care services offered to the community, especially to women and children, through attention to the effect of the organization's design on the motivation, morale, and effectiveness of the agency's professional, clinical, and administrative employees.

She is committed to the use of innovative teaching methods, such as case design, experiential learning, and service learning, as compliments to the use of traditional textbook and other teaching materials. This casebook is an example of her interest in the application of theory to the improvement of health practice.

Dr. Bender earned her PH.D. from The American University and her MPH in Health Policy and Administration from The University of North Carolina.

HEATHER MANNING is currently an internal consultant in the Office of the Division President at Kaiser Health Plan and Hospitals in Oakland, California. Since joining Kaiser in 1998, she has worked on projects in areas such as hospital strategy, leadership development, organizational restructuring, workforce development, hospital operations, and finance.

Ms. Manning earned a Master of Healthcare Administration degree at the University of North Carolina at Chapel Hill. During her graduate program, she worked closely with Dr. Bender on the initial concept and framework for the casebook. She also provided editorial and research assistance in developing the approach of the book and the actual cases.

Ms. Manning has also worked at Low & Associates in Chevy Chase, Maryland, where she worked on marketing research projects for the U.S. Public Health Service, National Health Service Corps, Manor HealthCare, and the National Science Foundation.

JULIE CURKENDALL received a Master of Health Administration degree in the Department of Health Policy and Administration at the University of North Carolina at Chapel Hill in 2000. She received her undergraduate degree in Health Policy and Administration from the same department in 1998.

She has worked with Dr. Bender as a graduate teaching assistant and actually took the undergraduate level course in "Organizational Theory and Behavior" under Dr. Bender's instruction in the fall of 1997. As a result, Ms. Curkendall has had experience with the preparation of the casebook as both a student writing and reviewing cases in a course setting and as a colleague working with Dr. Bender to develop the present casebook.